A BOOK OF NEWTON ABBOT

'A comprehensive, easy to read, and essential reference book ... will certainly merit a place in my collection and is a must for anyone really interested in the past and present of Newton Abbot.'

from a review in the Mid-Devon Advertiser

'This very authoritative and interesting work – welcome both for the enjoyment derived from reading it and also for the considerable amount of historical knowledge to be absorbed from its contents... This book must be assured of a permanent place in any bookshelf or library as a continual source of pleasure and of reference for future use.'

from a review in Devon Life

Cover: Detail of Newton Bushel, 1810, by George Shepherd, reproduced by kind permission of The Ashmolean Museum, Oxford. Note former St Mary's Chapel on left, St Leonard's Tower in middle distance, Seven Stars pub sign on right (the last demolished 1980)

St. Leonard's Tower, icon of Newton Abbot. Its nave was demolished in 1836 and the new St Leonard's built the same year, the roof of which can be seen in the right distance. Below it is the turreted corner of the former Half Moon Inn which was demolished, along with the Royal Oak next door, to make way for the opening of Newfoundland Way. The building beneath the gable on the left was formerly occupied by 'Ye Olde Bunne Shoppe', then the Vecchia Roma Restaurant and currently by the Tower Restaurant.

A Book of NEWTON ABBOT

Roger Jones

New revised edition

Ex Libris Press

First published in 1979
Revised and reprinted in 1979 and 1982
New edition 1986

**This revised, reset and expanded edition
published in 2006**

EX LIBRIS PRESS
16A St John's Road
St Helier
Jersey   JE2 3LD

www.ex-librisbooks.co.uk

Origination by Ex Libris Press

Printed by Cromwell Press
Trowbridge, Wiltshire

© 2006 Roger Jones

ISBN 1 903341 38 8

Contents

Prologue	7

1 Fragments of History

Early Times	13
Newton Abbot and Newton Bushel	15
Teignwick Manor	16
Wolborough Manor	17
King Charles I's Visit to Forde House	19
Prince William's Visit	21
Local Government	25

2 Geology

Rocks and Landscape	29
Building Materials	37
Wolborough Iron Mine	38

3 Traditional Products

Wool and Cloth	40
Leather	44
Cider and Beer	46
Ball Clay	50
Lignite	58
Books	60

4 Trade and Communications

Route Centre	63
The Market	64
The Newfoundland Trade	68
The Contribution of the Templers	70
The Railway	73

5 The River Lemon 79

6	**John Lethbridge: Famous Son**	87

7	**Views of Newton Abbot through the Twentieth Century**	91

8 Newton Abbot see in Old Maps

The Town Survey of 1843 — 103
The Ordnance Survey of 1888 — 106
1907 and after — 109

9 Church and Chapel

Highweek Parish — 113
Wolborough Parish — 115
Beginnings of Nonconformity — 119
Prebyterians, Congregationalists and Baptists — 120
Methodists — 121
Other Denominations — 122
The Established Church — 123
Since 1918 — 123

10 Some of the town's institutions

Schools — 125
Almshouses — 127
The Workhouse — 129
The Hospital — 133

11	**Newton Abbot Public Library & Passmore Edwards**	136

12 Town Trails

1 Highweek — 146
2 Wolborough — 149
3 Industrial Newton — 151

Bibliography — 153
Index — 156

PROLOGUE

It was 1976 when I came to Newton Abbot to take up the post of Divisional Librarian. This book was first published in 1979. I left the town the following year. There was to be a reorganisation of the County's library service which meant that Newton Abbot would lose its Divisional status; that is, the library at the centre of a network of nine branch libraries stretching from Kingskerswell to Chagford. Such a change would clearly have robbed my job of much of its interest and variety. There was the possibility of applying for a post higher up the hierarchy but that would mean forsaking the library environment with its agreeable mixture of books and borrowers and being walled up in an office to shuffle paper, or so it seemed to me.

A Book of Newton Abbot, which I published in July 1979, sold well from the outset. So much so that I had to arrange for a reprint after just six weeks. In the meantime I was working on a second book, *Rambles Around Newton Abbot*, a book of walks from villages in the countryside surrounding the town. This came out in spring, 1980.

My wife and I had often contemplated the possibility of running our own bookshop. This, together with the notion that I might write more books and develop a small publishing business, coincided with the threat to my job. We decided, with mixed feelings and after only four years, that it was time to move on.

In the summer of 1980 we migrated to Bradford on Avon in Wiltshire where, for 25 years until 2005, we ran Ex Libris Bookshop and I published more than a hundred books under the imprints Ex Libris Press – books on the West Country and country life – and Seaflower Books – titles on the Channel Islands. In 1982 I reprinted, for a second time, *A Book of Newton Abbot*, and in 1986 prepared a new revised edition, so that 5,000 copies have been produced in total though the book has been out of print for many years.

Having sold Ex Libris Bookshop in 2005 (and reached the age of 60) my mind turned to various projects which I might usefully pursue in my new-found state of semi-retirement. I had always recalled those four brief years in Newton Abbot with much affection. Living there had opened my eyes to so much and, ultimately, had altered the course of my life.

Back in 1976, before I could sort out a house for my wife, myself and our four year-old twin boys, I commuted to the library from my tent at a camp site in Daccombe. It was in June of that long, hot summer of 1976 so scarcely a hardship. Indeed, those first three sunny months in South Devon seemed like an extended holiday. There was so much new to discover and Newton is perfectly positioned as a base for trips to the seaside or to the moors.

Our boys spent four happy years at Bearne's Primary School in Queen Street, then under the headship of Mr Matthews. Having revisited Newton Abbot in 2006 to research this new edition, I was delighted, if a little surprised, to find that all three of the town's old-established, town-centre primary schools – Bearne's, Marsh and Wolborough – are still open for business. There is undoubtedly much to be said for small schools, even if they do not possess the very latest facilities.

It was those four years in Newton which opened my eyes to the fascination of place – both the built environment and the countryside – and of the relevance of history. To climb up to Wolborough and Highweek churches, then to look down on the town and beyond to the hills and valleys, is to contemplate a living geography and history text book. One can understand why Newton Abbot is situated where it is, how the various lines of communication reach it, how local industries developed and impacted on the town. In addition, there is a remarkably varied geology within a few miles radius, a fact which is reflected in the surrounding scenery and in the building materials evident in Newton's townscape.

I have paid occasional visits to the town since 1980, often in connection with publishing projects. We published two books (*Tall Ships in Torbay*, 1986; *Iron Horse to the Sea*, 1987) written by my former boss, the late John Pike, once Area Librarian of South Devon and based in Torquay. In 1990 we published *History of Teignmouth* by former colleague and Teignmouth Librarian, the late Grace Griffiths. In the meantime I revisited favourite haunts and compiled a book of walks entitled *Betwixt Moor and Sea: South Devon Rambles* (1987). These are a few of the books on West Country subjects which we published throughout the 1980s and '90s, most of which are now out of print.

Prologue

Unsurprisingly, Newton Abbot has undergone many changes in the intervening years. Like all English towns, a collection of retail sheds has sprung up on the periphery: TESCO on Newton Road (opened in 1982) on the low-lying land north of the town and B&Q on Jetty Marsh Road (opened 1998), for example. Another is Sainsbury's (formerly the Co-op, opened 1989) on the hotly disputed site at Pennin which was gifted to the town as a place of leisure and once sported an open-air swimming pool and park. The Dyrons Pool opened in 1989. The Globe Hotel, originally a coaching inn, on the corner of Courtenay and Bank Streets, closed in 1988 and now houses an extension of Austins, the town's own department store, demonstrating that the new out-of-town sheds have not succeeded in draining all life from the town centre. Madge Mellor's, that traditional and highly individual tea shop and bakers in Queen Street was taken over by Carwardines in 1987, but closed down only four years later. Today the premises house branches of Blockbuster Video and Burger King!

Newton Abbot, rumour has it, once boasted the greatest concentration of town centre pubs in the country. Whether true or not, it is remarkable how many pubs, mostly small, local and fairly traditional, still occupy the town's oldest thoroughfares – Bank Street, Highweek Street, Wolborough Street and East Street. And the Cider Bar lives on, one of only a handful of hostelries (four at the last count) dedicated to the traditional drink of the West Country. The 'Scrumpy and Western' website enthuses about 'Ye Olde Cider Bar' in Newton Abbot as follows: 'Entering the bar is like stepping back thirty or forty years – the decor is what would now be called minimalist, with no carpets and wooden stools and settles.... Stretching back from the main bar area is the famous Long Bar, home of the Cork Club which has held regular outings for its members since the early 1900s. Photographs of members past and present cover the walls.' The first occasion I visited this bar, in 1976, a cinefilm of a Cork Club outing was being shown in the Long Bar. It was packed with locals who recognised the faces, many long gone to a cidery grave, of past Club members.

The large number of surviving pubs is perhaps the more surprising in the face of the huge-by-comparison (and evidently very popular) new Wetherspoons outlet which has opened in Queen Street, known as The Richard Hopkins. The Wetherspoons chain has a policy of their pubs reflecting something of the character of the communities in which they are situated, perhaps to lend them local credibility. Richard Hopkins, we are reminded, was a local baker who made good. He once owned this corner of Queen Street and the adjoining lane is named after him. One has to hand it to Wetherspoons for doing their homework: the walls inside The Richard Hopkins are adorned with displays dedicated to various aspects of Newton's history.

The widening of Halcyon Road in 1992 to act as an inner relief road had a beneficial if somewhat temporary effect on traffic flows in the town centre. At the time of writing, a large area opposite the library is undergoing redevelopment. The hope is that the new ASDA superstore, so close to the town centre, can only benefit the rest of the town's traders. Any measure which will ease the town's traffic problems would be a blessing but one fears that this latest scheme will merely shift the bottlenecks slightly further from the town centre. However, the pedestrianisation of Courtenay Street, of Bank Street and of Wolborough Street from St Leonard's Tower to Newfoundland Way, as well as the more recently created Highweek Way, has transformed some of the town's busier and more attractive streets and made them more amenable.

During my visits to the town in 2006 I have walked everywhere. Newton enjoys a great location – you need only climb any of the town's encircling hills to be convinced of this. The town is often derided as being dull and workaday but I would disagree. Apart from the obvious attractions of Forde House and Bradley Manor, Newton Abbot is a great showcase for that icon of English towns: the terraced house. Consider Devon Square and the Abbotsbury area. Granted, some of the streets which climb the hill from East Street and Torquay Road could have been a little less meanly constructed in terms of garden and road space, but they possess a robust, if utilitarian, character which is not unattractive. And then there are the splendid villas, particularly around Courtenay Park and perched on Wolborough and Knowles Hills, which lend the town a certain distinction.

Newton Abbot Civic Society was founded, not before time, in 1997. Its introductory leaflet states that it 'exists to preserve and protect all that is best in our community, to improve amenities and to prevent encroachments and developments that might spoil our environment. The Society acts as a neighbourhood watchdog, but also goes much further and seeks to be actively represented where the interests of our community may be affected.' So more power to their community elbow!

Until my visit in January 2006, I did not know of the existence of Philip

Prologue

Carter's recent book on the town, published by Mint Press of Exeter in 2004. If I had then I may have been discouraged from preparing this new edition. Carter's is a very good book and I have enjoyed reading it. However, his treatment is primarily chronological; mine is most definitely thematic, and the themes I dwell on are mainly those for which I have a personal enthusiasm. There is inevitably some overlap between the two books but I feel they are sufficiently different in content and style to coexist happily. In addition to Philip Carter's book there has been a steady stream of compilations of old photographs over the past twenty years which are always interesting, if sometimes repetitive.

When *A Book of Newton Abbot* came out in 1979 I did not anticipate such a positive response; it was indeed a heartwarming experience. I thought local folk might resent an incomer writing about their town after only being here for the proverbial five minutes. But no, people approached me and thanked me heartily; 'Newton Abbot deserved a book to be written about it, and you've done it!' was the predominant sentiment.

I trust readers will forgive me for this lengthy prologue but it is hard to avoid a certain reflectiveness, if not nostalgia, in revisiting the place which kickstarted my modest publishing career.

Many local people, almost all then elderly, helped me with the first edition of this book. I feel sure that, by now, most if not all of them will have passed on, so there seems little purpose in repeating their names here in acknowledgement. I have spent many hours in the much improved town library working through its file of cuttings from local newspapers, checking editions of the *Transactions of the Devonshire Association* published over the past 30 years and anything else in the local history room which seemed promising. I am grateful to personnel at Teignbridge District Council, to Rod Tuck, Town Clerk of Newton Abbot and to old Newton friends Dave and Julie French for answering my many queries. Finally, my special thanks to Felicity Cole, Curator of Newton Abbot Museum since 1989, for encouraging me to produce this new edition and for her generosity in permitting me to include new illustrations drawn from the Museum's archives.

Roger Jones
September 2006

A

HISTORY

OF

NEWTON-ABBOT and NEWTON-BUSHEL.

AND ALSO, ILLUSTRATIONS

OF THE

Antiquities, Topography, and Scenery

OF

THE CIRCUMJACENT NEIGHBOURHOOD,

INCLUDING

Teignmouth, Torquay, and Chudleigh.

By The Rev. D. M. STIRLING.

"Where'er futurity may lead the way,
Where in this vale of Life I chance to stray,
Imagination to thy scenes shall turn,
Dwell on thy charms, and for thy beauties burn.—
And the last dream of Earth, that meets my eyes,
Shall be thy lawns and groves, and azure tinted skies."

NEWTON-ABBOT:

PRINTED BY W. F. FORORD.

1830.

Title page from the first book on the town, written by Rev. Donald McNee Stirling (a Scotsman perchance?) and published in 1830. The front endpaper of my own copy of this rare book is inscribed by the author as follows: 'A Gift to Mr Spiller, Collyford, from his Friend, Stirling, May 9, 1834.' Stirling was a schoolteacher in Newton Abbot who moved to Colyton in East Devon where he served as headmaster of the Grammar School from 1834 until he died in 1863.

1

Fragments of History

Early Times

Our corner of Devon has been inhabited by man for thousands of years. Flint tools used by Neolithic Man have been found at Berry's Wood Hill Fort near Bradley Manor. A brief description of the hill fort is given in **TDA** 1950 in which it is described as a contour hill fort with defences comprised of a stone rampart, now mostly demolished, and a ditch; two entrances at opposite ends give access to an enclosed area of about 11 acres and traces of huts inside have been found.

Milber Down Camp, although for many years referred to as a Roman Camp, was excavated in 1937-38 and was proved to date back to the first century BC. Bronze ornaments and articles of pottery were unearthed and can be seen at Torquay Natural History Museum. The Romans advanced into Devon in AD 47-48 and utilised the defensive position at Milber Down Camp. A number of Roman coins have been found in the vicinity of the Camp and part of a Roman pavement was found at the top of Milber Pine Woods.

The next oldest site near Newton Abbot is Castle Dyke at Highweek. Castle Dyke House in Highweek Village contains a Norman arch which leads to Highweek Hill. The hill is capped now by a clump of firs but shows the remains of a Norman castle, scheduled as an ancient monument. This castle was constructed on the motte and bailey layout: a deep ditch or dyke enclosed a circular space on which earth excavated was piled up until a high mound or 'motte', flattened at the top with steep sides, had been formed. On this was built the castle, probably of timber. In recent times a Norman silver coin was dug up in the garden of a house on the

Ashburton Road. The coin was minted during the reign of the Conqueror's son, William II. There are several wells in the gardens of cottages on Highweek Hill which probably once supplied the occupiers of the castle. The owners of Teignwick Manor (as it was then known), possibly absentee landlords, would have stayed at the castle when visiting their domain.

Highweek Castle may have been built as a defence against indigenous Saxons or as a lookout fortress for enemies coming by sea. The village of Teignwick grew up around the castle and the old chapel which stood on the site of the present All Saints Church; a chapel existed here at least as early as the thirteenth century. As the need for defence lessened, so did the need to maintain the castle and the hill-top settlement. When the Manor House at Bradley was established in the thirteenth century, the Lords of the Manor encouraged the growth of industry and settlement on the north side of the Lemon, which river formed the boundary of the Manorial Lands and the Parish. Thus Teignwick became Highweek, 'the village on high ground', to distinguish it from the growing settlement in the Lemon valley. Some authorities maintain that this lowland settlement was known as *Schireborne Newton* and others that *Schireborne Newton* lay on the Abbots' side of the Lemon.

Certainly Teignwick Manor occupied land to the north of the Lemon in the Hundred of Teignbridge whilst Wolborough Manor occupied land to the south in the Hundred of Haytor. Sometime after the Domesday Book, which was completed in 1086, both Teignwick and Wolborough Manors fell to the Crown. The Manor of Teignwick was granted by Henry II to his butler, Lucas, whilst Wolborough was later granted by Richard I to one William Brewer. In 1196 William Brewer granted the Manor of Wolborough, with the advowson of its church, to Torre Abbey which he had founded. In the meantime, north of the Lemon, Lucas of Teignwick had sided with the Norman barons in their revolt against the Crown and in 1205 the Manor was resumed by King John, who granted it to the widow of Lucas' grandson, Eustachia de Courtenay. Later still, by 1234, Henry III had granted Teignwick to Theobald de Englishville, a Norman knight who owed the King service in return for his lands.

Fragments of History

Newton Abbot and Newton Bushel

Wolborough Manor originally consisted of St Mary's Church on Wolborough Hill and a village to the west of the church in the vicinity of Wolborough Barton. Some authorities suggest that Wolborough Barton itself marks the site of an ancient Manor House. Ford Grange was an important farm and there was also a mill. This was probably Keyberry Mill, which was reputed to date from Saxon times: the Domesday Book lists a mill worth 5/- in the Manor of Wolborough. An article in **TDA** 1934 records that, at that time, the mill was still working to process maize and barley. Keyberry Mill was finally demolished in 1972.

At the beginning of the thirteenth century, the recently founded Torre Abbey was trying to increase its income and granted leases for building houses on the south bank of the Lemon. In 1220 Henry III granted the Abbots of Torre a charter for a weekly market, to be held on Wednesdays, and the right to hold an annual fair on the eve, feast and morrow of St Leonard, i.e. 5th, 6th and 7th November. St Leonard's Church, of which the tower now only remains in Wolborough Street, was built by 1350 when it is mentioned in a document. The weekly market was held on land on the west side of this church. At this time too, Teignwick Manor prospered and in 1246 Theobald de Englishville was granted a similar charter to hold a weekly market, on Tuesdays. Teignwick's market was held on a triangular shaped piece of land on the summit of a small hill behind St Mary's Chapel, which became known as Triangle Hill. This was corrupted into Tringle Hill and eventually into Treacle Hill. Theobald de Englishville left his Manor to his nephew and adopted son, Robert Bushel, in 1262. Robert died in 1269 and the Manor was inherited by his son, Theobald Bushel. By the end of the thirteenth century both communities and their markets were flourishing. It is recorded that Wolborough Manor had become Torre Abbey's richest possession. It was in the fourteenth century that these two expanding communities, divided by the River Lemon, became known as Newton Abbot and Newton Bushel. The two 'new towns' were thus distinguished by their owners, the Abbots and the Bushels.

Teignwick Manor

In 1309 the Bushels were granted a charter for two great fairs, each to last for four days, on the feast of the Ascension and that of All Saints, and in 1331 received a second charter for the weekly market henceforth to be held on Wednesdays. The Lords of the Manor were also granted the right to control the prices of bread and ale in their domain and the right to sentence convicts to death. The gallows were sited at Forches Cross (Forches is derived from *furcae* which is Latin for gallows). By the fourteenth century Newton Bushel had two watermills: Sherborne Mill was situated in the town and was probably a corn mill, and there was another mill at Bradley, outside the town. The leather and wool trades began to grow in importance and Newton Bushel developed as an important route centre. The town was on the road midway between Exeter and Dartmouth and was a convenient place for travellers to rest.

The Manor House at Bradley dates from the thirteenth century when it was begun by the Bushels; it then superseded the manorial home of Castle Dyke in Highweek. The estate remained in the Bushel family until 1402 when it passed through the female line to the Yardes. The Yardes of Bradley prospered as Newton Bushel prospered. Richard Yarde was the most distinguished of the Yarde family and was appointed Sheriff of Devon in 1442-43. In 1428 he built All Saints Church in Highweek. Richard Yarde and his wife Joan built most of what today comprises Bradley Manor; in 1429 they were granted a licence to add a chapel. In 1448 the Lords of the Manor built a chantry chapel at St Mary's in Highweek Street and also, at this time, beautified St Mary's Church in Wolborough: the arms of the Yarde family can be seen in the north aisle.

Bradley Manor was inherited in 1467 by Gilbert Yarde. At this time the estate contained four mills, to which Gilbert added a further two, making three fellmongering mills and three corn mills. The Yardes continued as lords of the manor until 1751 when it was sold to Thomas Veale, a wealthy lawyer, who left it to his nephew Thomas Veale Lane. He in turn left Bradley to his son Richard Lane, who was responsible for the rebuilding of Newton Abbot market as well as the alterations to old St Mary's Chapel. Richard Lane sold Bradley in 1841 when it was bought by the Reverend Frederick Wall. It was last sold in 1909 to Cecil Firth, the Egyptologist, who was descended from a Yarde, Susanna, who married out of the family in the seventeenth century. The present owner occupier, who gave Bradley Manor to the National Trust in 1938, can therefore claim to be a descendant of the Yarde family.

Bradley Manor

I have not given a very detailed history or description of Bradley Manor, or of the Bushel or Yarde families and more recent owners because there are full accounts of these given in a booklet on the Manor written by the present owner, published by the National Trust and currently available. Bradley Manor is open to the public on Tuesday, Wednesday and Thursday afternoons between Easter and September.

Wolborough Manor

Torre Abbey was dissolved in 1539, during the reign of Henry VIII. One John Gaverock was the Abbots' steward, a kind of medieval property manager, who supervised the Manor of Wolborough; for this post he received an annual salary of £3. Before the dissolution there were two courts in Wolborough, a civil and an ecclesiastical one. The former was at the 'Manor House' (built 1534) in Wolborough Street (home of the *Mid-Devon Advertiser* since 1990) whilst the latter was near the parish church, possibly on the site of the present Wolborough Barton, as already mentioned.

In 1545 the King sold the Manor of Wolborough to John Gaverock and his wife Jane, for the sum of £592.14s.2d. When Gaverock became lord of the manor he set about building himself a new manorial home at Forde; the former Manor House in Wolborough Street was used as servants' quarters. The older part of Forde House is the gabled annex at the back of the main building, as it exists today. After a visit to Devon by the King's Heralds, he was referred to as John Gaverock of Forde. Forde is so called because the hamlets of Forde stood where the roads to St Marychurch and Combeinteignhead crossed the Aller Brook at a fording place.

Forde House

John Gaverock's three daughters inherited Wolborough Manor and, in 1610, sold it to Sir Richard Reynell of the Middle Temple, an eminent lawyer and officer in the Court of the Exchequer and son of the Lord of the Manor of West Ogwell. He married Lucy Brandon whose father was Chancellor of the City of London. Sir Richard built the present Forde House, dated 1610, which adjoins Gaverock's structure. It is constructed in the shape of a letter 'E', probably in honour of Queen Elizabeth, who

Fragments of History

had just died. The grounds of Forde House were once much more extensive than they are today, and included the whole of the area now known as Decoy, so called because wildfowl were decoyed there to supply winter larder for the occupiers of Forde House. Part of this area now forms the Decoy Country Park, with a lake at its centre, thus returning the area to leisure use. There was also a deer park which was destroyed by the inroads of the railway. Forde Leat, which was originally constructed to drive the waterwheel at Keyberry Mill, was used to supply a lake dug in the grounds of Forde House.

Forde House is, architecturally, a plain, substantial structure built of rough-casted stone in the Elizabethan style. The main features of interest inside the house are the finely carved panelling, the oaken staircase and the massive oak doors and, above all, the magnificent ceilings, with much renaissance ornament on them, the lower ones flat and the upper ones coved. Several of them are extremely beautiful. Perhaps the most chaste of all is the one in the dining room, where broad interlacing bands of leaf ornament enclose square and diamond shaped forms to cover the entire surface and a frieze thirty inches in depth is studded with oblong panels within scalloped plate borders.

The arms of the Reynell family were formerly displayed above the entrance porch and can yet be seen in stained glass in the hall, together with those of later occupiers, Waller and Courtenay. In the drawing room, the arch above the southern window contains the sculpted arms of Reynell impaling Brandon, thus giving equal honour to both families.

King Charles I's visit to Forde House

King Charles I visited Forde House on September 15th, 1625 and stayed for some days. After visiting Plymouth to review the fleet he returned to Forde on the 21st, when he attended service at Wolborough Church. Richard Reynell of West Ogwell (cousin of Sir Richard Reynell of Forde House) and his brother Thomas were knighted by the King on his return visit. **Stirling** records that on the first visit many provisions were sent in for His Majesty's entertainment, a great proportion of which consisted of presents, and that on the second visit the list was even longer. Perhaps it does not cast much light on the history of Newton Abbot, but

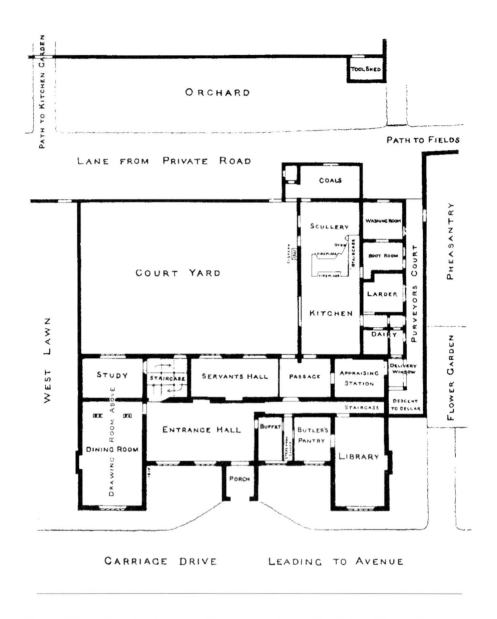

Sketch Plan of Forde House and its surroundings: Sir Richard Reynell's manor house, built in the shape of a letter 'E', adjoins the older manorial home at Forde, built some years earlier by John Gaverock

Fragments of History

I reproduce here that list because it is of interest in itself and shows the remarkable range of foods consumed by certain of our ancestors:

'A buck, a doe, a hunted tagge (a doe of a year old), a mutton, killed and dressed.

The fish consisted of eight score mullets, three dozen and a half whiting, four salmons, seven peels, seven dories, twenty one plaice, twenty six soles, forty eight lobsters, five hundred and fifty pilchards, etc.

Among the fowls and game, sixty nine partridges, five pheasants, twelve pullets, fourteen capons, one hundred and twelve chickens, four ducks, six geese, thirty seven turkeys, sixty nine pigeons, ninety two rabbits, one barnacle, one hernshaw, twelve sea larks, eleven curlews, twenty one dozen and half of larks, one heath pult, two nynnets, six seapyes, one stone curlew, four teals, three pea hens, and two gulls.

Six oxen, five muttons, two and half veals, besides several entries of ribs of beef, quarters of mutton, chines, tongues, sides of lamb, and a Westphalia gammon.

The liquor – two hogsheads of beer, one barrel of canary wine, and thirty five quarts of white wine. The entertainment cost £55.5.0.'

This must surely have been the greatest feast that Newton Abbot has ever witnessed! Thomas Reynell, as the King's server, had to sample the multitudinous dishes to make sure none were poisoned.

Sir Richard Reynell died in 1633 and Lady Lucy in 1652. In the meantime, their only daughter, Jane, married Sir William Waller, the parliamentary general, who succeeded to the ownership of Forde House. Sir William and Lady Jane's daughter, Margaret, married Sir William Courtenay of Powderham and the estate in turn passed to the Courtenays; Margaret presented Sir William with nineteen children. On 24th January, 1648, during the ownership of the Courtenays, Forde House gave shelter to Colonel Fairfax and his lieutenant-in-command, Oliver Cromwell, on their way to lay siege at Dartmouth, then being held by Royalist troops. Some authorities maintain that, during the Civil War, Forde House was besieged several times and that Waller, aided by Fairfax, finally captured it.

21

Prince William's Visit

William, Prince of Orange, sailed from the Hague in Holland and landed at Brixham on November 5th, 1688.

The progress made by the Prince and his army was slow because heavy rain had made the roads difficult. However, on November 7th he reached Newton Abbot and the Prince's intention to become King of England was proclaimed for the first time. It was market day in Newton and the declaration was read to the crowds from the tower of St Leonard's Chapel in Wolborough Street. The octagonal stone in front of the tower bears the following inscription:

> 'The first declaration of William III, Prince of Orange, the glorious defender of the Protestant religion and the liberties of England, was read on this pedestal by the Rev. John Reynell, rector of this parish, 5th November, 1688.'

We may note first, that the date given is inaccurate by two days and second, that it is almost certain that it was not the Rev. John Reynell who read the declaration. According to Macaulay's account in his *History of England* it was the King's Chaplain who was responsible. Whatever is the exact truth, we can be certain that this first address by England's future King was proclaimed in Newton Abbot. Copies of the documents were presented to representatives of Newton Abbot and Kingsteignton and then the bells of St Leonard's were rung to welcome the new deliverer and future monarch, King William III.

Prince William proceeded to Forde House where he found that the owner, Sir William Courtenay, was 'not at home'. Although the cautious Sir William had left instructions to his staff to provide food and accommodation for the Prince, he had decided not to welcome him personally. He supported the Prince's mission but Sir William reasoned that if it should fail, he should not find his own neck at risk. Prince William stayed in the small room over the porch, known ever since as the 'Orange

Opposite: One view of Prince William's visit to Newton Abbot, perhaps not entirely historically accurate!

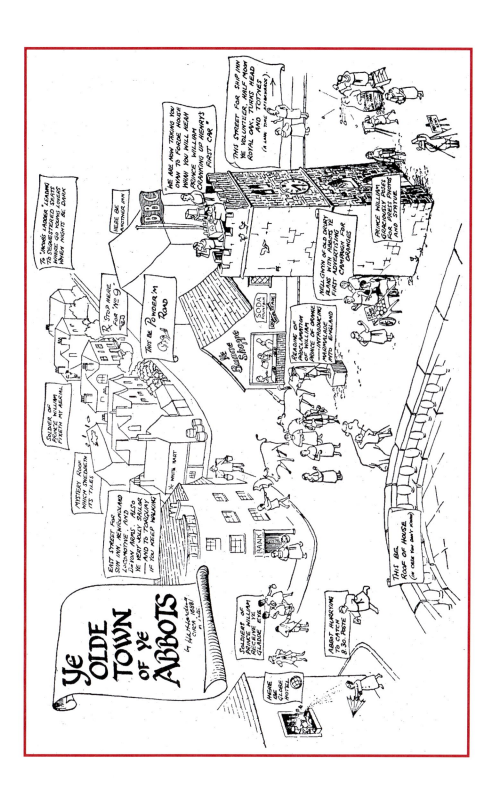

A Book of Newton Abbot

Room' and for many years decorated in that colour.

During his stay the Prince's artillery was stationed on Milber Down, once used by the invading Romans, and his army on the adjacent Aller Brake. A description of the Prince and his army, as they commenced their march to Exeter, is given in **Rhodes** and is surely worthy of quotation, such an awe-inspiring spectacle does it present:

> 'In the van were the Earl of Macclesfield, and 200 horse artillery, accoutred and mounted on Flanders steeds, with head pieces and 16 body armour, and attended by 200 negroes, wearing embroidered caps with white fur and plumes of feathers. Then followed 200 Finlanders in bearskins, with black armour and broadswords; and after these 50 gentlemen and as many pages to attend the Prince's banner, which was inscribed, 'God and the Protestant religion'. Then came 50 led war horses, preceding the Prince, who was mounted on a white charger, and wore complete armour, with a plume of white ostrich feathers in his helmet, and 42 running footmen by his side. He was attended by 200 gentlemen and pages, who were mounted. These were followed in succession by 3,000 Swiss, 500 Volunteers, 600 Guards, and the remaining part of the army, numbering in all about 30,000.'

Stirling records that a meeting was called at St Leonard's Chapel on November 5th, 1828, for the purpose of petitioning Parliament against the claims of the Roman Catholics of Ireland for emancipation. A petition was drawn up, signed and forwarded to both Houses of Parliament. It was probably not coincidental that this meeting was called on the supposed date, November 5th, and that Prince William's first declaration was read at the same spot. **Stirling** also records that, on November 28th of the same year, the Protestant cause was celebrated by a public meeting held in the town.

Members of the Courtenay family lived in Forde House until 1762 when it was let. From 1860 it was occupied by Mr J W Watts who held the office of High Sherriff of Devon in 1890. In 1960 when it became the base for an antique business and was thus used until 1978 when it was purchased by Teignbridge District Council for the sum of £76,000.

Fragments of History

I was asked to write a leaflet on Forde House to mark the visit of Queen Elizabeth II in 2nd April, 1980 to inaugurate the renovation of Forde House. This I did, though I misspelt 'commemorate' with four ms which went unnoticed and led to the entire print-run being scrapped and hastily reprinted. However, a genuine scholar, one Mary O'Hagan, was commissioned by Teignbridge District Council to write a comprehensive history of Forde House. This was published in 1990. It is a fine piece of work, attractively presented with copious illustrations. In it, the author tells the stories of the various families and individuals associated with the house, which makes a fascinating account.

Following the visit of Queen Elizabeth II on April 2nd, 1980, work on the renovation of Forde House progressed steadily and today is well looked after. The District Council's new offices are discreetly situated behind the house. The house itself is used for meetings and receptions and makes a splendid venue for its thriving trade in civil weddings and today the house and grounds are more accessible to the public than they have been for many years.

Local Government

'The first meeting of the Local Board for the Parish of Wolborough constituted under the Local Government Act, 1858, was held in 1864. In 1894, the Local Government Board gave their sanction to the change of name from Wolborough Local Board to Newton Abbot Local Board. The Urban Sanitary District became the Urban District of Newton Abbot, under the provisions of the Local Government Act, 1894 . . . In 1900, the Devon County Council made an Order, confirmed by the Local Government Board in 1901, extending the boundaries of the Urban District of Newton Abbot so as to include the Parish of Highweek and the parish of Milber, the latter being a new Parish taken out of the Parish of Haccombe-with-Combe.'

The above paragraph is taken from a petition of 1926 calling for Borough status for Newton Abbot. From it we can see that the organisation of local government in Newton Abbot began with the formation of

Wolborough Local Board. One of its first actions was to threaten to oppose renewal of the Totnes Turnpike Trust Act. Until 1868, Newtonians wishing to use Ransley Quarry had to pay 6d toll at the toll house beyond Mackrell's Almshouses in Wolborough Street. The Trust, however, removed the turnpike gate to the site of the present Wolborough Hospital on condition that the Board kept the road in repair from the site of the old gate out to the new turnpike. A new turnpike house was erected there and was used until the expiration of the Act.

Soon after the Wolborough Local Board was constituted, a local board was formed in Highweek. These two local boards continued to operate on opposite sides of the Lemon for many years – Wolborough representing the people of Newton Abbot and Highweek those of Newton Bushel. After much opposition from the Highweek side, the two local boards combined to form the new Urban District of Newton Abbot, and the ancient town of Newton Bushel merged with its larger sister town across the Lemon. The 1926 petition contained some 38 paragraphs, most of which emphasised the importance of Newton Abbot and listed the many services for which the Urban District Council was responsible. The final paragraph reads as follows:

> 'Your Petitioners believe that the granting of a Charter of Incorporation will lend to the great advantage of the town, and would lead to the promotion of its best interests, by giving it a higher and more efficient form of local government, and ensuring the stability of all its institutions, by fostering a civic spirit in the town, and encouraging the more willing and efficient performance of public duties, both by the inhabitants of the town and their elected representatives, and by giving to the town the additional dignity and influence which its past history, its growing prosperity, and its position in Mid-Devon would appear to justify.
>
> Your Petitioners, therefore, most humbly pray that Your Majesty may be graciously pleased, in the exercise of your Royal Prerogative, to grant a Charter of Incorporation, creating the Urban District of Newton Abbot a Municipal Borough, and to extend to such Borough and the Inhabitants thereof, all the powers and provisions of the Municipal Corporations Acts. And your Petitioners will ever pray.'

Book plate from the Passmore Edwards Public Library, as used before local government reorganisation in 1974, depicting the Newton Abbot coat of arms. It symbolises the amalgamation, in 1901, of the Urban District of Newton Abbot and the Highweek Local Board.

The right hand shield represents the Parish of Highweek, or the town of Newton Bushel, and has three bushels signifying plenteousness.

The left hand shield represents the Parish of Wolborough and has three symbols, each of which is associated with the church. One is the mitre, signifying dignity, another is the lamb, signifying sacrifice and the third is the tower, signifying strength. The two pastoral staffs on the shield probably refer to the Abbots of Torre.

A Book of Newton Abbot

This petition was, in fact, never submitted and Newton Abbot Urban District Council remained in existence until the Local Government Act came into operation in 1974. Under this Act a three-tier system of local government was established throughout Devon in which powers are shared among local parish or town councils, district councils and Devon County Council. Thus Newton Abbot UDC lost most of its powers to Teignbridge District Council which also incorporated the Urban Councils of Ashburton, Buckfastleigh, Dawlish and Teignmouth, the Rural District Council of Newton Abbot and part of the RDC of St Thomas, Exeter. Newton Abbot UDC was succeeded by Newton Abbot Town Council which, while it adopted the same boundaries as the old UDC and has the right to annually elect a Mayor, enjoys only the lowly status and minor powers of a parish council.

Newton Abbot Town Hall became redundant with the demise of Newton Abbot UDC. It stood in Courtenay Street and was demolished in 1977 to make way for Market Walk. The town hall was originally in part of a Wesleyan Chapel which had been built in 1848. Some twenty years later a new chapel was built on the opposite side of the street and the recently formed Wolborough Local Board purchased the disused chapel for use as a town hall. The original building was extended to provide accommodation for the town clerk, the treasurer and other officials. On the first floor was situated the council chamber and courtroom. At the rear of the building were, at one time, a constable's house and cells for offenders. Newton Abbot Town Council at first moved to temporary accommodation in Sherborne Road but since 1977 has rented offices in Brunel House in St Paul's Road. A new courthouse has been built in Newfoundland Way and was opened in 1978.

2

Geology

Geology is about rocks, and the rocks of any locality determine the soil, building stone and minerals to be found there. Rocks also greatly affect the shape and structure of the landscape. Thus it may be seen that an understanding of geology is necessary to a fuller appreciation of the physical and human environment. My own interest in the subject developed when I studied it at school more than forty years ago. It lay dormant for about a decade but greatly revived when I came to live in Newton Abbot.

The area's geological make-up is remarkably varied. This is due to major disturbances in the earth's crust with strata being folded and faulted so that one series of rocks is often found lying unconformably next to another. In addition, sedimentary rocks have been invaded by molten igneous rock from deep in the earth's crust which has generally solidified as layers or sills along bedding planes in the strata. And there are so many opportunities to see rocks exposed at the coast, in river valleys and in old quarries that it is impossible to ignore the area's geological make-up when one is out walking.

Rocks and Landscape

From the geological map – Newton Abbot Sheet 339 published by the Geological Survey of Great Britain – we can discern that the land to the south-east of Newton Abbot, between the Teign Estuary and Aller Vale and beyond, is composed of Permian rocks which are overlain on the west side by Eocene Aller Gravels and Cretaceous Upper Greensand. The Aller

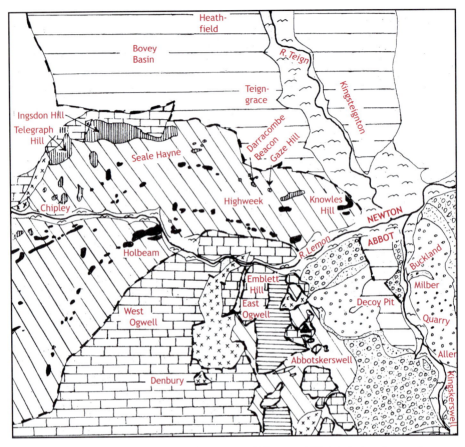

Simplified Geological Map of Newton Abbot and District showing main rock formations

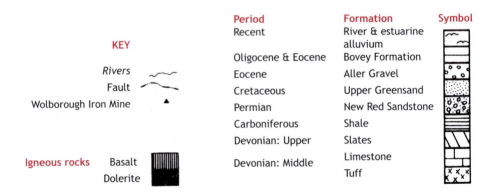

Geology

Gravels are exploited in the workings on the east side of the main road between Milber and Aller at the Royal Aller Vale and Zig Zag Quarries. The overgrown spoil heaps opposite Wolborough Barton in Coach Road mark an old pit which occurs in the same formation.

The rocks of the Permian Period, or the New Red Sandstone as they are sometimes collectively known, are actually composed of sandstones, clays, breccias and conglomerates. All these rocks are a deep red colour, so distinctive of many parts of South Devon where they occur and even of strata other than Permian, where solutions derived from the New Red have invaded underlying rocks and coloured them. The red colour is due to a concentration of iron compounds in these rocks, which were originally deposited in arid desert conditions.

Most of the land to the south-west of Newton Abbot is composed of Devonian Limestone. The western boundary of this outcrop follows a line from Chercombe Bridge, on the Lemon, south-west along the course of Blackford and Barham's Brooks. These streams flow along the line of a fault where Devonian Limestone has been thrust up against younger Devonian Slates. Volcanic ash, or tuff, is occasionally interbedded with the limestone strata. Tuff can be seen just to the west of Ogwell Lane where the River Lemon cuts through both limestone and interbedded tuff.

The Devonian Limestone has been worked and is still being worked at a number of sites to the south-west of Newton Abbot. The disused Ransley Quarry can be found at the south-east corner of Emblett Hill just north of the East Ogwell Road. This is a particularly interesting locality because the natural slope of the hill is fairly precipitous, owing to a fault which has caused younger, less resistant rock to slip down against the limestone. The softer rock has been eroded to leave a large block of limestone standing along the west side of the fault line. The face of the limestone has remained fairly intact owing largely to the absence of running water cutting into its surface.

Limestone is a pervious rock and rain falling on its surface sinks straight through. It is significant that the plain-like summit of this hill is easy to traverse in the wettest weather and that many springs occur at its base. Water percolating through the rock eventually meets an impervious stratum and emerges from the ground. There is a spring easily seen on the south side of the East Ogwell Road. The house 'Undercleave' which here lies in the shadow of Emblett Hill is aptly named. 'Undercleave' is sited on the impervious but easily eroded shales of the Carboniferous Period.

The Lemon Valley in Bradley Woods is a good place to view outcrops of Devonian Limestone. If you follow the riverside path from Ogwell Lane towards Chercombe Bridge you will find two limestone quarries. Both quarries may be spotted from the path by keeping an eye for the exposed rock face through the branches, or by looking for the remains of the quarries' accompanying lime kilns. The limestone here was evidently not worked for building stone but to produce lime for agricultural purposes. The kiln at the first quarry is rather dilapidated and overgrown but its hopper-shaped container is still discernible.

At the second quarry there is a fine lime kiln, with an outlet at its base on two sides, from which the burnt lime could be extracted. It is possible to climb to the top of the kiln and see down through it to the twin outlets below. The brick lining of the kiln is still pretty well complete. Much of Devon suffers a dearth of limestone or any lime bearing rock and farmers valued lime as fertiliser before artificial substitutes became generally available. I wonder how extensive this lime burning industry in the Lemon Valley was and how far afield its products were traded? It is certainly on record that lignite from the Bovey Formation was brought here to be burnt in the lime kilns.

Another interesting feature to be seen in the limestone of the Lemon Valley in Bradley Woods, this time on the south side near the path between Bradley Manor and Ogwell Lane, is the so called Puritans' Pit or, as it now seems to be known amongst some of Newton Abbot's schoolchildren, Devil's Pit. It was the place where the dissenting Reverend William Yeo held secret services for his nonconformist followers. A local schoolboy has told me that it is where witchcraft is now practised!

Some old guide books explain that Puritan's Pit was once a quarry but I find it hard to believe. It is not shaped like a quarry; the shape it displays – basically a hole in the ground – would hardly facilitate the removal of blocks of stone. It is quite an impressive hole and it is worth clambering down the rough path to its lowest point. From here you can see massive chunks of limestone lying one upon the other in the most haphazard manner. There are also the remains of trees which have crashed down from the edge of the woods above. It is impressive to look skywards through the circle of trees above which, because you are at about the level of their deepest roots, seem extraordinarily tall. I would say that Puritans' Pit is a

Geology

collapsed cavern. That is, an underground cavern once existed in the limestone, probably owing its formation to the passage of an underground river which dissolved the rock. There came a point when the cavern grew so large that its walls were unable to support the overhanging rock and...crash! Indeed, there are many hollows leading off from the deepest corners of the pit to be seen today. Perhaps there are underground chambers as extensive as those of Kent's Cavern in Torquay.

So, generally speaking, the elevated country to the south-east of Newton Abbot consists of Permian strata, partly overlain by the Aller Gravels and Upper Greensand, e.g. Milber Down and Wolborough Hill, whilst that to the south-west consists of Middle Devonian Limestone with interbedded tuff. Under the town and each side of the Ashburton Road, in a widening arc, are to be found rocks of the Upper Devonian Period. This formation consists of slates, shales and mudstones but, most typically, slates. I have read somewhere that the broken slates are known locally as shillet. The slates are relatively soft and easily eroded and tend to produce a low-lying landscape, except where these strata are reinforced with hard igneous rocks such as dolerite.

An indication of the underlying rock is often given by the colour of the soil in a particular locality. In Powderham Park the soil is quite red and as you descend the hill by Powderham Road you are, in fact, passing through a succession of Permian strata. In the town itself the earth is black. This is due to the alluvial deposits in the flood plain of the Lemon. On slightly more elevated ground, say the Abbotsbury area, the soil is grey rather than black. Anyone who has the doubtful good fortune to possess a garden here, as I did, will know by hard experience how difficult it is to dig: the soil is very clayey and this clay is derived from the underlying slate, fragments of which are found about a foot down.

Stirling lists one Mr WC Radley: Mineralist, in his directory of local tradesmen. In a book called *The Panorama of Torquay* by Octavian Blewett, published at about the same time, a paragraph from the section on Newton Abbot reads as follows:

> One of the principal attractions in this town is the Mineral Museum of Mr WC Radley, a diligent labourer in the field of scientific research. To his exertions the Geologist is indebted for the discovery of trilobite in *grauwacke* of Knowles Hill.

33

Grauwacke is a German term for slate and trilobite is one of the earliest forms of life in the sea, the fossil remains of which are occasionally found in ancient sedimentary rocks.

Knowles Hill owes its existence not to Devonian Slates which comprise its lower reaches but to hard igneous rocks which reinforce its top and middle. This once molten rock is not granite like the igneous rock of Dartmoor, but dolerite. Dolerite differs from granite in its chemical composition, i.e. the minerals it contains and, more obviously perhaps, in its colour and structure. The colour of dolerite is generally dark, almost black, often greenish, depending on the minerals present. It has a finer appearance than granite, particularly the massive, crystalline granite of Haytor. Dolerite is crystalline, like all igneous rocks but, because it has cooled and solidified more quickly than granite its crystals are smaller and often invisible to the naked eye. The Dartmoor Granite is a vast upwelling of once-molten rock; the dolerite of Knowles Hill is a small intrusion, or sill, which was rapidly cooled by the surrounding country rock.

There are quarries in Knowles Hill. There is one to the south of Jetty Marsh Lane. This quarry, as far as I can make out, is utterly overgrown and inaccessible. There is also one on the summit of the hill which is lost in private land. However, there is a wealth of evidence to be seen among the rocks used in the walls on and near Knowles Hill. There are massive black, grey and greenish rocks which are various forms of dolerite and its close relatives. There are also spotted slates, the spots representing compositional changes in the slates caused by the contact made with the molten dolerite. In the wall on the left side of Knowles Hill Road as it descends to Kingsteignton Road there are many pieces of rock which are very dark and pitted with tiny spherical holes. Such holes are sometimes found in intrusive igneous rocks such as basalt and represent gas vesicules.

A notable feature of the landscape west of Newton Abbot are two chains of hills. It is enlightening to compare a geological map of this area with a contour map in order to discover their geological basis. The first chain can be said to start at Knowles Hill and runs due west through Gaze Hill and Darracombe Beacon in Highweek and culminates in Ingsdon Hill at 612 feet and Telegraph Hill (at Bickington) at 639 feet. All these hills are capped with dolerite or, more commonly, basalt. Similarly, a second chain can be said to start at Hangman's Hill, south of the Broadlands Estate and continue westward through unnamed hills south of the Ashburton

Geology

Road. The River Lemon cuts a fairly steep valley between dolerite capped hills north of Morley Farm; these culminate in the elongated hill north of Holbeam Farm.

Like Knowles Hill, all the hills in these two chains survive as hills because of the protective capping of a relatively hard igneous rock. This is either dolerite, which has been intruded in sills between rock strata, or basalt which has been extruded from volcanoes. In both cases the igneous rocks are found interbedded with the slate formation and, like the volcanic tuffs already described, were formed contemporaneously with the surrounding sedimentary rocks.

South of Telegraph Hill, near Chipley, is a disused quarry where volcanic basalt was once worked for road metal. This is pillow lava, so called because its appearance resembles a mass of pillows. This is the characteristic of lava which has been extruded under the sea. Concentric rings of gas vesicules can be seen in the split pillows. These vesicules represent escaping gas which was trapped as the molten rock cooled and solidified. They are sometimes filled with minerals and the pillows themselves are sometimes veined with quartz.

There is another major geological formation of considerable importance and that is the Bovey Formation of the late Oligocene and early Eocene Periods. This formation is of comparatively recent antiquity: 25-30 million years old. The Bovey Basin to the north and north-east of Newton Abbot is a flat, diamond shaped tract of land which measures approximately seven by three miles and is bounded by higher land on all sides and to the south-east by the Teign Estuary. An excellent view of the full extent of the Bovey Basin and the ball clay workings may be obtained from the elevated footpath on the north side of Knowles Hill. This path can be reached at the end of Rundle Road or from Seymour Road (see page 151). During the late Oligocene Period this natural depression, formed by earthquake activity along the line of the Sticklepath Fault which passes through Devon from north-west to south-east, was a lake fed by rivers which flowed from the uplands of Dartmoor.

These rivers contained materials which were deposited as sediments in the calmer waters of the lake. The lake took millions of years to fill and a cross section of the strata in the Bovey Basin shows that the lake bottom sank under the weight of the sediments deposited. The thickness of the deposits grows to 3,500 feet in the centre of the basin around Heathfield.

35

The Bovey Formation consists essentially of clay and lignite with smaller quantities of sand and gravel. The clay is known as ball clay, the raw material of which is derived from the rotted granite of Dartmoor, and is the result of weathering and the subsequent chemical and physical decomposition of the feldspars, the main mineral constituent of the granite.

The china clay of south-west Dartmoor and Bodmin Moor has a somewhat different genesis to that of ball clay. There the granite has weathered into clay *in situ* and the hydraulic method of extracting clay is employed. This allows a clay-bearing slurry to be transferred to tanks where the clay content is isolated by settlement. The refining process is not necessary on the same scale in the Bovey Formation because the clays here have been transported from their parent rock by water to be graded by the natural process of deposition in the lake into which the water flowed. Thus ball clay is, in many respects, purer, or more refined than china clay and exhibits certain properties peculiar to itself.

Lignite, on the other hand, is of organic origin. It is a carbonaceous substance midway between coal and peat and is formed by the partial mineralisation of vegetable matter. William Pengelly, the great Cornish geologist, did much pioneering work on the fossil remains of plants and trees found in the Bovey Lignite. At the time of the deposition in the lake which once filled the Bovey Basin, Dartmoor was some 3,000 feet high and covered by a sub-tropical forest of huge coniferous trees, resembling the giant sequoia which grow in California today. Vines clung to the trunks and branches of these trees and there was a dense undergrowth of huge ferns. Traces of this exotic flora can be found in the lignite. Vegetation was carried downstream into the lake, particularly in times of heavy rain when great floating rafts of vegetation eventually became waterlogged and sank to the lake bed. This is why the seams of lignite are thickest at the north-west end of the Basin, whilst the finest of the clay material was carried furthest to the south-east corner and why, everywhere in the formation, beds of pale sticky clay are interspersed with beds of dark woody lignite.

Ball clay has been used to make everything from bricks to porcelain. The economic significance of the Bovey Formation is discussed in Chapter 3: Traditional Products.

Geology

Building Materials

The variety of rocks around Newton Abbot gives the town a corresponding choice of building materials. Until the present century the Devonian Limestone was the source of much of the building stone used, either as random pieces or as worked blocks of various shapes and sizes. The limestone you see in Newton Abbot varies in colour from pale to dark grey and can be of a uniform appearance or veined with crystalline material of varied hue; the veins are generally white with pinky red tints. The variation in the appearance of the Devonian limestone is very localised and differs not only from quarry to quarry but also from different levels within the same quarry, depending from which level a particular block is extracted. Devonian limestone quite often contains fossils; these are corals or small shells. The walls of St Leonard's Church (now Antiques Centre) in Wolborough Street is a good place to spot a coral bearing limestone.

The exterior of the Alexandra Theatre and Market Hall provides an excellent display of Devonian Limestone in a pristine state. Much of it is veined with white and pink. Such veins represent solutions, generally calcium carbonate, which have crystallised in joints and cracks in the rock. It is the same substance which furs up kettles and pipes in hard water areas. The colours present are generally due to impurities. The pinks and reds are most likely iron compounds derived from the Permian rocks which once overlaid the limestone.

Many of the older domestic dwellings of Newton Abbot were built of limestone although the stone was often rendered. This was done because the limestone does tend to hold damp and whilst this was perhaps acceptable in churches and public buildings it was not so in the up-market villas built on the hills around Newton Abbot. The Devonian Limestone lends the town a distinctive character although in recent years many fine stone buildings demolished to make way for featureless concrete and standardised brick. Mackrell's Almshouses in the Totnes Road and the old Workhouse in East Street are two fine examples of the Devonian Limestone used as a building stone. One fascinating feature of this rock, or at least of some examples of it, is its ability to change colour. St Mary's Church, Abbotsbury, appears almost completely grey in dry weather but, after rain and a good soaking, positively glows pink!

By the turn of the century locally manufactured bricks seem to have overtaken worked limestone as the most popular building material, no doubt because of their comparative cheapness. It was at this time that many of Newton Abbot's brick terraced houses were erected. Slates were worked in the lower quarry on the north side of Knowles Hill. Large chunks of slaty rock can be seen used as building stone in the front garden walls of the terrace of houses in Cricket Field Road, and were probably obtained from this lower quarry. Large quantities of roofing slate were worked at quarries south of Bickington, near Down and Wickeridge, and no doubt these were the source of much of Newton Abbot's slate. There are few examples of slate hung walls in Newton Abbot although there is a group of cottages in Old Exeter Road whose end walls are slate hung and one or two backs and sides of old buildings in Highweek Street. Road metal was obtained from hard igneous rock such as the basalt at Chipley Quarry.

There is a fair amount of Haytor Granite to be seen around the town. It is used chiefly in those parts of a structure which require the strongest and most hard wearing stone. The doorstep and the plinths each side of the entrance to the library are of granite. The famed Watcombe Clay, used as the raw material in the old Torquay Potteries, is a Permian rock. Permian breccias are sometimes used as building stone but are more commonly seen in Teignmouth and Paignton, although there is some to be seen in the door jambs of the main entrance to Wolborough Church, as well as in the church's Norman font. Massive flints can be seen piled on top of brick built gate posts outside many houses of the Edwardian era, for example in Abbotsbury Road and Church Road. These flints, derived from the chalk of the Cretaceous Period, are found in the Aller Gravels of Milber Down and Aller Brake. They represent the resistant residue of a thick deposit of chalk which once overlay South Devon.

Wolborough Iron Mine

Newton Abbot once had an iron mine which, it is recorded, produced 1,240 tons of brown haematite during the years 1872-73. Wolborough Iron Mine was dug into the hill between Wolborough and Abbotskerswell, a little south of the present cemetery in Totnes Road and opposite the road to Denbury.

Geology

One Augustus Anthony Smith spent a holiday in Newton Abbot where it was brought to his attention that the slopes of this hill contained a reddish-brown stone which was much heavier than normal stone. This hill was known to Newtonians as Firestone Hill which suggests that sparks flew when horses shod with iron passed over it or, perhaps, when the stone was worked with iron tools. Mr Smith found that this heavy red-brown stone was brown haematite which contained a high proportion of iron.

He invited his three partners, who together controlled 'The North of England Iron Company', based at Workington, Cumberland, to inspect his find and to discuss the possibility of exploiting the iron ore. The decision was soon taken to go ahead and on March 6th, 1872, the company secured a 21 year lease from the Earl of Devon to sink a mine at Wolborough, on payment to the Earl of 1/- per ton of iron ore sold or extracted. H Beare and Son, Engineers of Liverton (and later of Newton Abbot) supplied the rails, trucks and other ironmongery and a steam engine was installed to lift ore to the surface.

A mining engineer, one William Henry Hosking, was appointed mine captain. He lived at 77, Wolborough Street whilst he was working at the mine. Mr Hosking was paid on a sort of piece work basis of so many shillings per fathom excavated. He was responsible for hiring men and encountered no problems in finding experienced miners since many were employed not far away in the metal mining region on the south-eastern rim of Dartmoor. Eight men were taken on. They constructed trackways and a road, and built an engine house alongside a shaft which was dug to enable the iron ore to be mined. It took a little over a year to dig and bring to the surface 1,240 tons of brown haematite. When the deposit was exhausted Mr Hosking had been unable to find any other and the mine was closed.

Little evidence of the mine's existence remains today. The Earl of Devon had written into the lease that the mining company should return the land to its original arable condition when mining operations ceased. So it was that all surface buildings were demolished and spoil heaps levelled. Records show that the ore raised was loaded onto ships at Newton Quay, in batches of between one hundred and two hundred tons and taken to the smelters of South Wales.

3

Traditional Products

Wool and Cloth

In medieval times, Devon was one of the most important sheep-rearing counties. By the fourteenth century most of its towns had their own wool and cloth industries and Newton Bushel was no exception. As I have already mentioned in the initial chapter, early documents record the growing number of woollen mills in the town at this time. There were many tradesmen associated with the wool and cloth industries, such as fellmongers, fullers, dyers, spinners, weavers and tailors. Fellmongering is the process whereby the wool is removed from the sheepskins and fulling involves the cleaning and thickening of the wool prior to spinning.

Daniel Defoe, who travelled around Great Britain in 1724, recorded that Newton Bushel had an important serge industry at that time and that these serges were sent to Exeter for export to Holland. In 1739 the Government was debating whether to remove the export duty on Irish wool and cloth. The importance of the woollen industry is shown by the fact that several citizens of Newton Bushel sent a petition to Parliament against it. During the eighteenth century the annual cloth fair was described as the town's busiest fair.

There is an interesting history of Vicary's written by Charles Lane Vicary which was published in an issue of *The Vicarian*, the firm's magazine, in 1928. This article throws some light on the history of the wool, cloth and leather industries in Newton Bushel and gives some glimpses of the Vicary family, members of whom were so important to the economic life of Newton Abbot for many years. The Vicarys' presence in Newton Bushel was preceded by that of the Branscombe family. Samuel Branscombe

40

Traditional Products

Senior conducted his wool business from the building on the corner of Halcyon Road (site of the former White's Garage). The business failed and the owner sold out to the Vicary family, packed up his possessions and left town. Samuel Branscombe Junior owned a tanyard in Bradley Lane but was bought out by Moses Vicary in 1837, and thus started the Vicarys' involvement in the leather industry.

Aerial view of Bradley Mills

The Vicary family had been engaged in the wool trade in the sixteenth century in South Molton and Bideford and had a store at Denbury near Newton Abbot. The Newton Bushel wool business was founded in 1747 by Robert Vicary who also ran a fellmongers yard at Crediton. Robert married late in life and his son Moses was born in 1776. In 1786, when Moses Vicary was ten years old, the ailing and ageing Robert Vicary left the entire contents of his business to his son. His wife Elizabeth and young Moses then left Crediton and came on horseback to Newton Bushel. Elizabeth Vicary carried on the business until Moses was old enough to assume responsibility himself. Elizabeth Vicary died in 1843 aged 89 years.

In 1802 Moses Vicary married Rebecca Doke, the daughter of Gilbert Doke, and had a son Moses in 1804. Gilbert Doke had served an apprenticeship with a cordwainer in Totnes in the craft of making boots

Sorting wool at Vicary's

The pulling shop at Vicary's showing men pulling wool off sheepskins

Traditional Products

and shoes and afterwards came to Newton Bushel and built up a flourishing boot and shoe making business. In his article Charles Vicary states that 'much of the credit for the industrial development of Newton Abbot is due to Moses Vicary and his father-in law Gilbert Doke'. He also states that 'Moses Vicary was undoubtedly a business man of exceptional ability. Through the extraordinarily difficult period of the Napoleonic Wars and the still more difficult period that followed he steadily increased his commercial interests and his reputation for straight and honest dealing was known far beyond the borders of Devon'.

Moses Vicary Junior had five sons, all of whom were engaged in the wool and leather business. One of his sons, William Vicary, earned fame as a scientist and was a distinguished member of the Devonshire Association. He was one of the accepted authorities on Devonshire fossils and antiquities.

Vicary's wool and leather works expanded considerably in the second half of the nineteenth century, when the depression caused by the Napoleonic Wars and their aftermath was passed. In 1860 John Vicary purchased the ruins of Bickford's Paper Mills, situated at the top of Bradley Lane, which had been destroyed by fire some years previously. On this site a fellmongering and tanning mill were constructed. This was an addition to Bradley Mills which had been rebuilt in 1833, and were destroyed by fire in 1882. The factory was again rebuilt and can be seen today, though no longer used as a woollen mill. Set in the wall facing Bradley Lane is a plaque as follows: 'JV & S Rebuilt 1883', i.e. John Vicary and Sons 1883.

This John Vicary, like his father Moses, had five sons, four of whom were active in the business. In 1914-15 the first wool processing machinery was installed but again, in 1921, the mill burnt down. The mill was rebuilt and equipped for wool combing, twelve combs being installed. During the 1920s Vicary's employed some 700 hands, 300 of which worked in the tannery. The firm continued operation as an independent body engaged in tanning, fellmongery and wool-combing until 1939 when it became a subsidiary of Sanderson, Murray and Elder Ltd., of Bradford. Soon after the outbreak of World War II the fellmongering business was discontinued.

During the war the mills were kept occupied with Government quotas and after the war the factory began specialising in the processing of man-made fibres. Business declined until the works finally closed down in 1972.

Thus ended over two centuries association of the Vicarys with the wool and cloth industries of Newton Abbot, and a much longer tradition of the wool trade in Newton Bushel, stretching back at least to the fourteenth century.

Leather

The leather industry originally developed in conjunction with the wool industry. One significant product were waterproof boots for fishermen bound for the Newfoundland cod fisheries, many of whom were recruited in Newton Abbot and surrounding villages and embarked for their voyage from Newton Quay. The wool was removed from the sheep skins during the fellmongering process and the hides remained to be made into leather. Liming was the initial stage whereby hair was removed from the skins by steeping them in a lime pit which contained a mixture of lime and water. Tanning is the process whereby the raw hides are converted into leather. The term comes from the word tannin which is a substance derived from the bark of certain trees and is employed to make a solution in which the hides are immersed. Currying is an outmoded process whereby the leather was impregnated with grease in order to produce certain types of leather which were required to be strong, supple and waterproof.

With the wool industry, the origins of Newton Bushel's leather industry can be traced back to the fourteenth century. Local craftsmen connected with the industry included tanners, curriers, boot and shoe makers, glovers and saddlers. I have already mentioned Gilbert Doke, boot and shoe maker, who set up a business in Newton Bushel in the 1760s. Charles Vicary, in his history of Vicary's, states that among Doke's best customers were Henley and Sons, the cider manufacturers, for whom he seems to have made the entire supply of boots needed for their employees.

There was a good supply of raw materials for Newton Bushel's tanyards: skins from the town's slaughterhouses and fellmongers, lime from Bradley Woods, soft water from the Lemon and tannin from the bark mill which stood on the Mill Leat further downstream. Bark was imported to supplement the local supply which was obtained from the woods around Ashburton. The local demand for leather goods was inflated by the needs

Traditional Products

of travellers, especially for saddles and harnesses, and by the fishermen engaged in the Newfoundland Trade for strong, waterproof boots.

Vicary's leather business flourished in the second half of the nineteenth century and production increased. Vicary's produced the finest quality leather which was mostly used in the manufacture of shoes. In 1879 the Vicary family closed its tanning interests throughout the rest of Devon and concentrated production at Newton Bushel. Business continued to prosper in the early years of the twentieth century and the 1914-18 War created a great demand for leather. Vicary's were contractors to the Admiralty and the War Office and made harnesses and bandoliers for soldiers.

Tanning yards at Vicary's where hides were tanned by revolving in drums

The following description of work in the tanyards between the wars has been given to me by a former employee:

> 'Sheepskins, or basils (hence basil yard), were treated, with the wool on, by first soaking in water and then rolling to crush the burrs or seeds on a burring machine. Following this they were hung in chambers, virtually a brick cell with no lighting or ventilation, where they became hot by their own chemical decomposition, after which they went to the pulling shops

45

where the pulling of the wool was done by manual labour on a rounded board with a double handled knife. The skins then went to the liming yards to be treated by rapidly revolving them in the lime pits to restore them to their preheated condition. Later they went to the Basil Yard for treatment (with dog excrement which was brought in from local kennels) and tanning.

The larger tan yard (towards Highweek Street) was for hides, many of which were imported from South America and Australia. They were first dry salted and soaked in water pits. When ready they went through an unhairing machine. These had long rollers with brass blades similar to a turbine. The hairs, when removed, were saved for plastering in the building trades. When the hides were finished they were marked with a large acorn which was Vicary's trademark.'

Operations contracted after World War II and were eventually discontinued. Devon Leathercrafts, which had been operating in Newton Abbot since 1930, continued the tradition until its eventual demise in 1982, its former works in Kingsteignton Road now occupied by Blackler's Garage. Thus ended some six centuries or more of leather working in Newton Abbot.

Cider and Beer

Until the late nineteenth century most cider in the West Country was made on farms and cider making was for most farmers just one of their activities. However, the Newton Abbot district had one of the first commercial cider works to be established in Devon: Henley's Cider Company was founded in 1791. The Teign Cider Company was also founded in that year but began as merchants dealing in farmhouse cider and only later began producing cider and mineral waters.

Although no longer independent but part of the Beecham Group, until recently the Teign Cider Company still had its works at Netherton, on the Combeinteignhead Road. Here cider apples were crushed and fermented as they had been for two centuries, though of course not in the same

Traditional Products

primitive fashion. Until World War II cider was sent in bulk to London for blending and bottling. The London bottling plant was destroyed in the blitz and after that bottling was carried out at Netherton.

Henley's Cider Company had a factory at Abbotskerswell. Some twenty men were employed here to process cider apples which were grown either on the firm's five orchards at Abbotskerswell or by local farmers. A guide to Newton Abbot written in the 1920s quotes Henley's as having 21 refineries in South Devon, although no doubt the Abbotskerswell plant was the largest. Henley's also had a depot in Teign Road where their products were dispatched by rail to London where the firm had a branch. The Newton Abbot depot included a cooperage and a bottling plant and employed a further twenty men. It closed in 1933 when Henley's merged with Whiteways of Whimple which was founded in 1890 and is Devon's leading cider maker today. The Abbotskerswell plant continued in operation until 1965 when it closed down.

A little book was published in the early 1930s, punningly entitled, *A Pressing Invitation to Henley's Cyder Factory*, which was evidently given to visitors as it informs the reader, 'To guide you through one of the largest cyder factories in Devonshire'. At the Abbotskerswell works you could see the original cellars used by the firm in 1791, old presses dating from 1835 in which stone rollers were pulled by horses in a rotary movement, mills and press houses of 1884 and still in use in the early 1930s, maturing vats and cellars, and a view of the extensive apple orchards. The tour ended with a tasting of the famous cider and the guide book urged you to drink Henley's Cider 'for the good of your health, the delight of your palate and for the love of England', a neat bit of spin which suggests that drinking cider is a patriotic duty.

The health giving and hygienic attractions of cider were stressed in advertisements for Henley's products. Henley's did, in fact, win the Gold Seal Certificate of the Institute of Hygiene in 1932. It seems that cider had earned a reputation for quite the opposite qualities, if **Stirling**'s account of the subject is anything to go by:

> 'A very important part of the produce of every farm, is cider. The orchards are generally extensive, and excepting when the apple blossom happens to fail, immense quantities of this cooling beverage are annually produced. In plentiful seasons,

large cargoes of it are sent to London, although very little of it is used there as cider, and that little so adulterated that few Devonians can relish it; but it is for the most part sold to wine merchants, who best know to what purpose it may be applied. The Devonshire cider is supposed to possess as good a body as white wine – it has however, been accused of producing the gout, so prevalent in this county, and what is denominated the Devonshire colic. Chemical experiments tried at Alphington some years ago, gave rise to an opinion that our cider is the sole cause of the latter, by its being impregnated with the lead of the cider press; but this supposition, though adopted by persons of unquestionable learning and judgement, has been confuted, being inconsistent with evident facts.'

Henley's Cider is commemorated today, together with other matters of significance in the history of Newton Abbot, in the shape of a circular plaque, one of several inserted into the paving in pedestrianised Courtenay Street.

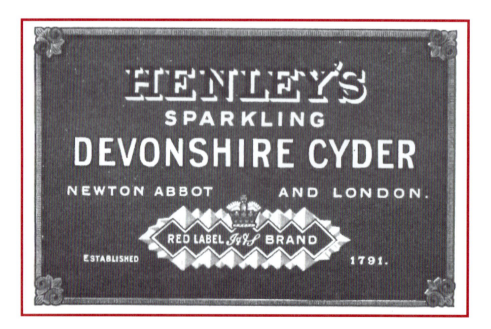

Traditional Products

However, it is doubtful that cider was universally popular in the West Country, except perhaps on farms where agricultural workers were at one time partly paid for their labours with cider. It seems that much of Henley's product was sent to London where, as Stirling tells us, it was not always sold as cider.

Beer was brewed in Newton: the 1843 Town Survey shows two breweries. The Palk and Pinsent Brewery stood at the corner of Mill Lane in the building which was formerly Branscombe's woollen mill and then White's Garage. A second brewery stood on the banks of the Lemon between Wolborough and Bank Streets; this is marked 'Old Brewery' on the 1843 Survey. In addition **Rhodes** refers to the Mills Brothers' Brewery in Wolborough Street.

An article in **TDA** 1881 refers to an alcoholic beverage called 'grout ale' which was brewed and drunk only by poor people who were known as 'grouters':

> 'They have in the West a thick sort of fat ale which they call grout-ale ! The grout-ale is sweet and medicated with eggs. A kind of ale different from white ale, known only to the people about Newton Bussel who keep the method of preparing it as a secret; it is of a brownish colour. However, I am informed by a physician, a native of the place, that the preparation is made of malt almost burnt in an iron pot, mixed with some barm [yeast] which rises on the first working in the Keeve [fermentation vessel] a small quantity of which invigorates the whole mass, and makes it very heady.'

If grout ale was consumed by poor people in need of some relief from the rigours of their daily lives, then the products of the town's breweries no doubt supplied the many inns and ale houses which lined the old thoroughfares of Newton Abbot.

Water for the Mills Brothers Brewery was drawn from the River Lemon, which is soft and contains a significant proportion of arsenic. The Palk and Pinsent Brewery's water supply came by a pipe laid underground from the hard water spring which issues into the Mill Leat at Bradley Manor. Hard water is better suited to the brewing process. We may

A Book of Newton Abbot

speculate that imbibers of the Palk and Pinsent brew not only enjoyed a better pint but also had a greater life expectancy.

The proprietor of Pinsent's Brewery was Mr. John Balle Pinsent, who was descended from an old Newton family and lived in Minerva House in Highweek Street, which is quite an impressive house inside and out, even today. Mr Pinsent enjoyed a profitable business: he kept two horses in his stables and had a large staff of domestic servants, gardeners and grooms. His garden was famous for its beauty; it included a lake fed by a channel cut from a southerly branch of the Mill Leat. His son inherited the estate and then his four children, who sold it to Devon County Council. In 1936 it was purchased by Newton Abbot Council and the gardens formed part of the extension to the cattle market which was opened in 1938. The house remains and is now occupied by Farm Accounts Limited.

The basic ingredient of beer is malt, derived from barley. Tuckers Maltings, housed in a fine range of buildings in Teign Road between the railway tracks, where it is served by its own siding, and Osborne Park, were built in 1900. It is a substantial structure, with walls some two and a half feet thick and with small windows designed to maintain an even temperature within. The firm began in 1831 in Ashburton and remains one of the oldest surviving independent agricultural companies in the country. The Newton Abbot premises constitute the only working malthouse left in the West Country. The works opened to the public in 1991 and are well worth a visit to see how traditional methods are employed to encourage the barley to germinate to produce malt. Beer remains the largest market for Tuckers malt. Indeed, the Teignworthy Brewery, which began in 1994 and shares the same building, uses Tuckers malt to brew its beers. Besides beer, Tuckers malt is used in whisky , and in products such as Horlicks and in some breakfast cereals.

Ball Clay

The occurrence and geology of the ball clay and lignite of the Bovey Formation have been described in an earlier chapter; here we are concerned with their economic significance.

It is said that the Romans were the first to exploit the soft, pale clay of the Bovey Basin, though this is hard to prove. We do know that the Bovey

Traditional Products

Clay was being dug to be used for making smoking pipes in the late seventeenth century, some fifty years before the discovery of china clay in West Devon. By the early 1700s pipe clay was being shipped from Teignmouth to many ports around the coasts of Britain. Josiah Wedgwood incorporated Bovey Clay in his specially blended pottery clays and his successful innovations ensured it a growing market. There were potteries in the vicinity of Bovey Tracey, one of which Wedgwood described as 'a poor trifling concern and conducted in a wretched slovenly manner'. New potteries were slow to establish themselves near the clay pits because South Devon could not provide the coal necessary for firing the kilns. It was cheaper to transport the clay to the Staffordshire potteries than coal to Devon. One reason why the products of the local potteries were so inferior was because the locally obtained lignite used for firing the kilns did not create a sufficiently high temperature.

The first clay was dug for local pipe makers by tenant farmers who rented land from the Cliffords of Ugbrooke, the Courtenays of Forde, the Templers of Stover or the Church. Clay merchants appeared on the scene and established a trade outside the immediate area. The first successful merchant was William Crawford of Dorset, who arranged shipments from Teignmouth to London. By the mid-seventeenth century, Liverpool's share of the clay traded by sea was more than half; this clay was destined for the Staffordshire potteries. Another clay merchant of this period was Nicholas Watts, one of the forerunners of Watts, Blake and Bearne.

By the close of the eighteenth century the trend in the clay trade was for individual merchants to cease to trade independently and to form partnerships, some of which eventually became the first ball clay companies. The name of Watts, Blake and Bearne first appears in the port books of Teignmouth in 1861. Watts, Blake and Bearne is now the largest ball clay producer in Europe, although it shares the market with English China Clays. WBB acquired the local firm of Hexter, Humpherson and Co. shortly after they acquired Candy and Co.'s clay getting and pipe making interests, including the Devon and Courtenay Clay Company, in 1964. WBB merged with Sibelco, a Belgian company, in 1989, when English China Clay sold its 20%+ share. The former WBB offices, in Park House overlooking Courtenay Park and Devon Square, were vacated in 2003 and are, at the time of writing, undergoing redevelopment as living accommodation. The WBB Minerals Group is an international company

Three pictures of the ball clay trade reproduced from the little book, Devon Clay, *first published in 1927 by the Devon & Courtenay Clay Co, Ltd. of Newton Abbot.*

Top left: Cutting the clay in an open quarry

Bottom Left: The mouth of a square pit showing haulage apparatus

Above: Loading the barges at Newton Quay to be floated downstream

and continues to be a major employer in the Newton Abbot area; its local headquarters are situated at East Golds Works on the Kingsteignton Road.

Candy Tiles, whose origins date back to the 1860s, merged with British Ceramic Tiles in the 1990s when their factory at Heathfield was entirely rebuilt. The company today employs more than 200 people and some ranges continue to be produced under the name Candy Tiles.

The bricks used in many of Newton Abbot's Edwardian houses are the products of Hexter, Humpherson and Co., whose works were situated in Kingsteignton Road. **Rhodes** quotes the company as employing 150 hands at the turn of the century.

The earliest method of clay extraction was to dig out lumps on one level, or 'course', somewhat similar to digging peat from a bog. Four specially adapted hand tools were used in this task: the clay spade, the lumper, the tubil and the pog. The clay spade had a 12-inch blade and was used to cut and cross cut the exposed clay surface into about 9-inch squares. The tubil was used to extract the first lump in a course and for trimming the sides of the excavation. The lumper was a form of mattock used to undercut and lever up lumps of clay partially cut by the spade. Finally the pog, which was an iron spike on a long wooden handle, was used to spear the cut lumps and lift them to ground level. Clay lumps, which measured about 9 inches square by 1 foot high, were somewhat perversely called 'balls' – hence ball clay, and weighed about 35lbs.

Later pits, which measured 24 feet square, were dug to allow more efficient exploitation of clay in a restricted area. These pits had vertical, timbered sides and reached a maximum depth of 80-90 feet, when the pit often had to be pumped dry of water. The clay was extracted in the same way as described above, except that the clay was generally hauled to the surface in a wooden bucket operated by a crane. Mines were sometimes dug, in the form of a rectangular vertical shaft measuring about 13 feet by 6 feet. At first, the area at the base of the shaft only was dug. Later it became more common to dig short, heavily timbered tunnels from the shaft bottom into the seam of clay for no further than about 100 feet.

The next major development in ball clay extraction came in the 1930s when Holman Brothers of Camborne, the Cornish mining engineers, devised a pneumatic spade to replace the old tubils for digging out the clay. This mechanical spade, powered by compressed air, was first used in 1932. In 1946 the Government ordered an enquiry into the ball clay

Traditional Products

industry which recommended that the industry be encouraged to mechanise. This was followed by a steadily increasing demand for ball clay at home and overseas and the pneumatic spade became widely adopted. However, this mechanical spade was only one aspect of a complete transformation of the ball clay industry which has taken place since the war.

Machines such as the hydraulic excavator and rotary bucket excavator have now replaced the pneumatic spade and make open cast working in large pits much more efficient. At the same time the development of working underground by the adit method has improved production in that area. Heavily timbered, vertical shafts have been superseded by driving tunnels directly into clay seams and working much larger areas at right angles to the main tunnel. The life of an adit mine is likely to be some 25 years, compared to only two years for the old shaft mine. There are now several adit mines in production, although open-cast working remains the cheapest and most important method of clay extraction.

Methods of clay extraction have been developing at the same time as modes of transport, a vital element in the trading of such a bulky commodity. In the early days, the clay was taken by packhorse to Teignmouth for shipment, or possibly by horse and cart. Clay cellars were built at Hackney as early as 1751. Once the packhorses brought the clay to this point, it could be stored under cover until ready to be loaded onto

The head of the Stover Canal where clay barges were built and clay was stored in cellars - note the heavily buttressed walls and chutes for loading the barges.

a barge bound for Teignmouth. The ruins of the bargemen's cottages can be seen by the footpath as it runs just west of the A38 road bridge and the Passage House Inn.

The very short Hackney Canal was constructed in 1843 by the Cliffords of Ugbrooke so that the clay could be loaded at Kingsteignton rather than Hackney. The rather longer Stover Canal was constructed in 1792 from the head of the Whitelake Channel as far as Ventiford; a terminal basin was constructed here, together with clay cellars. A further activity at Ventiford was the building of clay barges. Wharves were constructed at the head of the Teign Estuary. Just east of the main line railway bridge, at the confluence of the Teign and Lemon, there can be seen the massive, circular granite plinth in which was once set a capstan (see lower picture on page 53). Before the Whitelake Channel was cut to connect the Teign with the Stover Canal, the navigable Teign ended in a basin on what is now the site of the railway goods yard. Here there was another wharf used for the loading of clay onto barges.

Clay barge and salmon fishing at the head of the Teign estuary

The average dimensions of the wooden clay barge was 50 feet long by 14 feet wide and each took a load of 30 tons. The barges carried a single square sail which gave them an appearance resembling Viking ships. They

Traditional Products

were either blown by the wind or drifted on the ebb and flow of the tide to and from Teignmouth. With the advent of powered boats, clay barges were towed by tugs up and down the river. The advent of barges and canals greatly increased the tonnage of clay shipped from Teignmouth, although the passage along the estuary was difficult and in the early days the clay had to be trans-shipped in mid-stream. The New Quay was built by George Templer at Teignmouth in 1825-27 and this facilitated the transfer of clay from barge to ship.

The South Devon Railway linked Teignmouth with Newton Abbot in 1846, but the railway did not affect clay distribution until the construction of the Moretonhampstead branch line in 1866. The course of this new branch line followed the Stover Canal through the Bovey Basin and a siding was built in 1890 to facilitate clay loading at Teignbridge and another at East Golds clay pit in 1938. The Moretonhampstead Branch brought an increasing amount of clay traffic to the main line and this traffic increased particularly when the enterprising Great Western Railway took over the South Devon. From the 1930s onwards road traffic took an increasing share of the clay haulage business, although in 1965 British Rail began to fight back with its special clay liner trains from Cornwall and Devon to the Staffordshire Potteries which still operate successfully.

The ball clay industry today is highly mechanised and successful with most of its products being exported through the local port of Teignmouth. The vast bulk of the clay supplied to manufacturers of ceramics and to the chemical, rubber and plastics industries is not in the crude lump form but dried and pulverised or shredded and blended to a certain specification designed to meet the particular needs of users. According to an article in **TDA** 2000, the demand for ball clay is increasing and is unlikely to diminish. At the time production was approaching one million tons a year with Devon providing 80% of production mainly from the Bovey Basin deposits with smaller tonnages produced from the Petrockstowe Basin in North Devon, with 77% of the total being exported. Deposits are sufficient to maintain production and growth for very many years to come.

The finest clay in the Bovey basin occurs in the south-eastern margin and this is the area of most activity, although there are pits and mines in the centre and on the western margin. An isolated outcrop of ball clay is found at Decoy and this was worked as an open pit together with several mines for many years. It was closed in 1965 and allowed to fill with water.

57

A Book of Newton Abbot

Now known as Decoy Lake, it forms the centrepiece of Decoy Country Park, an amenity which provides opportunities for walking, sailing and various field sports as well as the Wolborough Fen Nature Reserve.

Lignite

The lignite of the Bovey Formation should perhaps not be included in a chapter dealing with 'Traditional Products' because, although many attempts have been made to exploit this substance and great hopes have been raised regarding its economic potential from time to time, it has rarely been successfully extracted and utilised. It is really a 'Traditional Non-Product' but it has an interesting history which is perhaps worth relating here.

As I described earlier, the ball clay occurs with alternating seams of lignite. The lignite is generally regarded as waste and it is this substance which forms many of the spoil heaps which surround the clay pits and mines. It is combustible and has been used as a fuel from time to time, usually in periods of scarcity. There have been, over the years, sporadic attempts to exploit this doubtful fuel on a commercial basis. Records show that such attempts began in the early sixteenth century.

I have come across some references to the projected use of Bovey Lignite. One was a scheme, in 1905, to electrify the Haytor Granite Tramway from Bovey Tracey to Haytor using power produced by producer gas which would be derived from 'Bovey coal'. Another failed plan was described in a guide to Newton Abbot published in 1920 as follows:

> 'It is anticipated that electricity will be produced in bulk …from the lignite deposits estimated at many millions of tons…so that subsidiary industries may be opened up to the advantage of the town and district…a Syndicate has been formed for the purpose of opening up on the banks of the River Teign an electrolytic refinery for the refining of copper smelted abroad.'

We can perhaps be thankful that the inferiority of the local lignite spared us the construction of a copper refinery on the banks of the Teign. In the

Traditional Products

1930s, in a guide produced by Newton Abbot Council and the local Chamber of Trade and Commerce, reference is made to 'the vast deposit of lignite near Newton Abbot – the largest in the world – is now being tapped successfully…and this will open another great industry as time goes on.'

An interesting booklet was written and published in 1947 by one C W Parish who at the time was Chairman of British Lignite Products Ltd. and had the support of Sir Stafford Cripps, President of the Board of Trade, to whom the book is dedicated, and the Ministry of Fuel and Power which, at the time, was desperately searching for ways to alleviate the fuel crisis. Mr Parish points out that the Bovey Lignite contains montan wax, a valuable commodity for which there were many uses in industry. Germany, with its vast resources of *braunkohle* (brown coal), or lignite, held a world monopoly in the production of this substance and in 1913 sent representatives to Bovey Tracey with a view to extracting the local lignite and shipping it to Germany for processing. The Germans left Bovey Tracey two days before the declaration of war in 1914 but before they did so they had built a small power station producing 100 h.p. which was fuelled by lignite and supplied the village of Liverton with electricity.

It was Mr Parish's declared intention that his company should build a plant at Bovey Tracey to extract montan wax (notwithstanding the fact that British scientists had discovered a substitute during World War II), as well as gas, petrol and oil from the lignite. At the time of writing the book, in 1947, production of raw lignite was some 100 tons per day, which was mixed with coal or coke and used as fuel. It was the company's plan to produce briquettes using the lignite residues after the extraction of montan wax. The forecast production was half a million tons per year which would be extracted from open pits and mines. The reserves were estimated at 50 million tons in the north-west corner of the Bovey basin where the seams of lignite are thickest. Briquettes were produced for a while but instead of being used for domestic purposes they were shipped from Teignmouth to the Channel Islands where they were used for fuelling glasshouse boilers.

At one time some large spoil heaps of lignite in the Kingsteignton area ignited by spontaneous combustion and remained alight for many years. The smell in the surrounding area was, I am informed, quite obnoxious! I have experimented with this ill-fated substance in my grate at home. The lignite smoulders rather than burns and certainly does produce clouds of acrid smelling smoke!

Books

When I published *A Book of Newton Abbot* in 1979 books could scarcely be considered one of the town's 'Traditional Products'. But now, 46 years after David & Charles published their first tome, books continue to emanate from Newton Abbot, notwithstanding the departure of prime mover David St. John Thomas in 1990. In fact, many hundreds of titles have appeared over the years, most with a distinctive character. Indeed, many people regard David & Charles and Newton Abbot as synonymous – in their minds it is books, and books from David & Charles, which distinguish the town. Pass through Newton Abbot by train or leave Newton Abbot by road and you are bound to see the old signal gantry – 30 feet high and 20 wide – which became redundant in 1987 with the installation of a new computerised electronic signalling system controlled from Exeter. It was acquired by David St John Thomas, moved from Newton Abbot Station and erected here like a flag to proclaim the presence of David and Charles. So it seems apt to include here some account of the D&C phenomenon. Besides, I am a provincial bookman myself so the subject is one which holds a certain fascination.

It was as fellow members of the Railway & Canal Historical Society that David St John Thomas and Charles Hadfield became acquainted. Charles had a background in publishing and David in journalism. Both had written books: David on railways and Charles on canals, respectively titles in the series 'Regional History of the Railways of Great Britain' and 'Canals of the British Isles' published by the Phoenix House. David and Charles decided to pool their talents and begin publishing themselves. Their imprint became known as David & Charles.

Their first publication was a booklet, *The Hay Railway*. By the time the company was incorporated, on 1st April, 1960, they had published three such booklets. Then came *Devon Flood Story*, an early bestseller which went though five printings: 21,000 copies in total and all printed in Dawlish. The centre of operations quickly outgrew the garden shed which David had erected for the purpose in his back garden. In 1964 the company moved to rooms above the booking hall at Newton Abbot Railway Station – a most apt location, considering the subject matter of many of their books. This was the year that Charles, twenty years David's senior, took a back seat and when D&C's list began to grow at an exponential rate, in one year publishing in excess of 300

Traditional Products

new titles. In addition to their own publishing programme, in 1971 David and Charles took over the Readers Union Book Club and turned round an enterprise which, at the time, was at a low ebb.

This rapid growth was checked by the 1973 oil crisis and the subsequent economic decline, then raging inflation. Nevertheless, the company built Brunel House on the other side of the tracks on the site of a row of railway cottages which had been destroyed in the 1940 blitz on the railway station. By 1975 all D&C's staff were relocated. D&C's growth coincided with the running down of the railway works which was fortunate for the employment prospects of people living in the area. The company very soon expanded into the former carriage and wagon repair shops adjacent to Brunel House. By 1981, when the company celebrated its 21st birthday, David & Charles had published more than 3,000 books, of which 1,000 were in print. The company employed up to 300 people and kept busy many local freelances, hotels and cafés.

D&C's starting point may have been railways and canals but the company quickly branched out into all manner of non-fiction subjects, often related to particular parts of the country or to quite particular subjects. They had a ready market in public libraries where a D&C title often precisely covered a relatively obscure topic which a borrower might enquire about. But for me, as for many booklovers, D&C's main strength remained in what David himself refers to as 'solid books of local interest'. David and Charles published many books which focused on a small section of the country, not necessarily the obvious places such as National Parks, or concentrated on a particular aspect of place such as their books on the industrial archaeology of a locality or the 'Geology Explained' series. These were books aimed at the proverbial intelligent layperson, written and presented in an accessible style, many of which are sought after today and demand surprisingly high prices in the second-hand market.

David wrote *Journey through Britain*, an unusual memoir which was published in 2004. In it he travels around the country visiting places, meeting people and recalling books with which he was associated at one time or another throughout the David and Charles years. Unashamedly self-indulgent, his book is a thoroughly enjoyable read, dealing, as it does, with those three features of a happy and fulfilled life: people, places and books. With characteristic enthusiasm, he writes of the D&C phenomenon as follows:

'The fact that I was a provincial, with an interest in nostalgic and practical subjects happened to coincide with the public's increasing appetite. In our early years books on railways and canals, industrial archaeology and local history, specialist collecting, gardening and needlecraft not only met with little competition but enjoyed a strong public library demand. So good were our sales that D&C quickly became a national and then an international institution.'

David St John Thomas left the D&C offices for the last time at the end of December 1990, having sold the company to Readers Digest. This was followed by a management buy-out, then a takeover by an American company. So books are still published and book clubs serviced in Newton Abbot, thus maintaining what has become a tradition.

David St John Thomas has lived in Nairn in Scotland for many years. It was he who suggested to Alison Shute, the then Devon County Librarian, that Newton Abbot Library might develop a railway collection to mark the fact that it was, or had been, an important railway town. In *Journey Through Britain*, David promises that 'My railway collection goes there on my death.' That is something all railway students will look forward to (the books, not the demise of their benefactor) but Newton Abbot Library will certainly have a problem adding any more volumes into its already bulging shelves.

4

Trade and Communications

Route Centre

Newton Abbot has been on a main highway at least since Roman times, when a road led south-west from Exeter, via Teign Bridge and Newton Abbot, through Marldon to Brixham and Kingswear, where there was a ferry over the Dart Estuary to Dartmouth. These coast ports of South Devon were busy places during the following centuries, acting as bases for alternately conducting trade and waging war with France, the dispatch of men to the Crusades and, in the Tudor and Stuart reigns, the comings and goings of merchant adventurers, explorers and buccaneers.

Of more local significance, the position of Newton Abbot at the head of the Teign Estuary and at the confluence of several valleys favoured the town's development as a trading centre for the surrounding area. By the seventeenth century roads had been constructed linking Newton Abbot with Totnes, Ashburton and Moretonhampstead. The Turnpike Acts of the eighteenth century provided an impetus for building new roads and for the improvement of existing ones. A new road was built to Torquay and beyond, starting in East Street. Tolls were collected at roadside tollhouses which were built on all the major roads out of Newton Abbot. Some of the last to be demolished were at Pennin and at the top of Highweek Street, at the junction of the Highweek and Exeter Roads. Tollhouses on the Exeter Road at Forches Cross and on the Kingskerswell Road at Longford can still be seen.

From the earliest times, Newton Abbot has been a town of much through traffic. There were many inns where travellers could stable their horses, refresh themselves and spend the night. Old town directories reveal

A Book of Newton Abbot

the large number of inns in East Street, Highweek Street and particularly in Wolborough Street where the market was held until it moved to its present site in 1826; these are described more fully in a later chapter. Kingsteignton Road, built on marshy ground and leading to Kingsteignton via a new road bridge on the Teign, was built by the Totnes Turnpike Trust by Act of Parliament in 1836. Before the new road was built, Kingsteignton could only be approached via the Exeter Road and Teign Bridge and must have been much more remote from Newton Abbot.

The railway could not cope with the slopes of Great Haldon in the way the Roman Road had and so followed the coast and approached Newton Abbot from the Teign Estuary. Eventually, railway branch lines were constructed and duplicated road routes to Chudleigh and Christow via the Teign valley, to Moretonhampstead via Bovey Tracey and to Brixham and Dartmouth via Torbay.

The Market

The development of Newton Abbot is inseparably linked to that of its market. As we have seen, the Abbots of Torre held a weekly market on land to the west of St Leonard's Church from 1220, whilst the Bushel family's market was held on the hill behind St Mary's Chapel from 1246.

The twin markets of Newton Abbot and Newton Bushel continued to be held side by side, though not without incident. In 1411 there was a dispute between William Michel, Abbot of Torre, and the burgesses of Newton Abbot which was heard at Exeter Assize Court. The Abbot attempted to sue the townspeople for, among other things, preventing the town's bailiffs from collecting the tolls and other profits made at Newton Abbot's market and fairs. The Abbot won his case but the court suggested that he should take a fixed rent for the market and fair tolls from the head bailiff.

Not much is known about how Newton Abbot market faired after the dissolution of Torre Abbey in 1539 but we do know that Richard Yarde of Bradley purchased the market and fairs of Newton Abbot and, in 1633, amalgamated its markets and fairs with those of Newton Bushel. The site of Newton Bushel market on Treacle Hill was abandoned in favour of the site of Newton Abbot's market in Wolborough Street. The new, larger

Trade and Communications

market continued to be held on Wednesdays. There were buildings in existence to enable some of the market trade to be conducted under cover and, in 1684, Gilbert Yarde built a butchers' market, although the cattle market continued to be conducted in the street. When Sir William Waller came to reside at Forde House he took legal action in an attempt to wrest the market of Newton Abbot from the Yardes of Bradley, but the Court of the King's Bench decided against his claim.

When Thomas Veale purchased Bradley Manor in 1751 he also acquired Newton Abbot Market. By this time a smaller weekly market was held on Saturdays, in addition to the regular Wednesday market. Three annual fairs were held: a cattle fair on June 24th, a cheese and onion fair on the first Wednesday in September and a cloth fair on 6th November. In 1817 Bradley Manor and Newton Abbot Market were inherited by Reverend Richard Lane, the grand nephew of Thomas Lane. By this time the buildings behind St. Leonard's Church in Wolborough Street were becoming inadequate for the expanding market, and Rev Lane built a new market on a piece of land called Lydes Meadow, which is where the present Market Hall and Market Walk now stand.

The new market buildings were completed in 1826 at a cost of £3,000 and **Stirling** comments that 'The various markets are ingeniously disposed apart from each other, and being all in one spacious area, must be very convenient'. However, 70 years later and 30 years after the demolition and replacement of Rev Lane's market buildings, **Rhodes** described them as follows:

> 'There was a potato or vegetable market with a shambles adjoining, and a detached building for the butchers. Over ¢he latter was a corn chamber, and as years went on the buildings became dilapidated, with the result that the dust caused by the people doing business in the corn chamber used to fall through the floor into the butchers' market, the meat, of course, not being improved thereby.'

Rhodes also recalls that one of the cattle sheds was used as a lock-up in which those found drunk and disorderly were incarcerated for the night, but that on one occasion an offender took up the pebble stone paving and dug a hole underneath the door by which he made his escape.

Newton Abbot Market from Drumclock Corner: Before the livestock market was moved (in 1906) to the north side of Sherborne Road.

Newton Abbot Market from Drumclock Corner during the mid-1920s.

Making room for the bus station, 1950

Trade and Communications

In 1867 the market buildings and the ownership of the market itself was purchased from Reverend Lane by the newly formed Wolborough Local Board for £8,000. The Board invited plans for a new complex of market buildings by public competition. **Rhodes** records that 'Some of the architects competing sent in fanciful designs providing for the deepening and widening of both the Rivers Teign and Lemon, and the extension of the Newton Quays right up to the Market, and shewing ships discharging their cargoes right into the market buildings!'

The Board eventually embarked on a rebuilding scheme for the market costing £15,000 which included the covering over of the River Lemon in the vicinity of the Market, the construction of new buildings and a road linking the Market to Courtenay Street. This work was completed in 1871. The new market buildings consisted of a pannier or butter market, with a separate building for the fish and vegetable markets, a new corn exchange and a public hall, the Alexandra Hall. The Alexandra can still be seen to bear the date 1871. In its early days the Alexandra was used for concerts, lectures, banquets and as a skating rink. It was later fitted with a stage for the performance of stage plays with seating for 600 persons; the Newton Abbot Repertory Company presented its first performance, 'The Importance of Being Earnest' in 1920. Later still the Alexandra was converted into a cinema.

After the 1871 redevelopment livestock was penned in the market square which later became a car park and now incorporated in the Market Walk Shopping Centre. In 1906 Newton Abbot Urban District Council acquired land to house the livestock market: cattle, sheep and pigs were now bought and sold in the area between Sherborne and Halcyon Roads. The cattle market was enlarged by the Council in 1938, as a plaque in the wall facing the Market Hall commemorates. The new cattle market includes land which had formed the extensive garden at the rear of Minerva House in Highweek Street. At the same time a new corn exchange was built on the site of Stockman's Mill. The layout of the livestock markets remains essentially the same today, although the buying and selling of sheep and pigs now takes place in the shadow of the multi-storey car park, constructed in 1972.

The livestock market continues to prosper with its weekly sale held on Wednesdays attracting traders from a wide area. Special sales include the Annual Sheep Sale which is held on the first Tuesday in August when

A Book of Newton Abbot

young lambs are brought down from the moorland farms and sold to lowland farmers, and the Annual Christmas Show of livestock and farm produce held on the first Monday in December. The separate fish market lost trade during the First World War when fish was scarce and closed down in the early 1920s. The building was converted into public lavatories and slipper baths and was finally demolished in 1977 to make way for Market Walk. Another part of the former market buildings here was utilised as a Fire Station before the present Station was erected at the junction of Kingsteignton Road and The Avenue.

The weekly market is Newton Abbot's oldest surviving institution, having been held every week for the past seven and a half centuries. It would be fascinating to find pictures of the old market in Wolborough Street, or of Rev Lane's market of the mid-nineteenth century, but do any exist? The Market Hall and Alexandra Hall happily survived the redevelopment, have been completely refurbished and continue to serve their original purposes.

The Newfoundland Trade

Sir Humphrey Gilbert, whose family had lived for generations at Compton Castle, near Marldon, was an Elizabethan adventurer who sailed to America. In 1583 he landed at what became known as St John's in Newfoundland and claimed 600 miles in every direction for the British Crown. Thus it was that Britain's oldest colony was founded. The British Government encouraged the development of the fisheries from the start, though not settlement. However, people did settle and by the early 1800s about 20,000 persons were living in Newfoundland. Many of these could claim descent from those early West Country fishermen.

Boats bound for the cod fisheries off Newfoundland set sail from many West Country ports each spring from the late sixteenth century, when the trade became established, until the mid-nineteenth century when it became uneconomic. The decade of maximum prosperity for the Newfoundland Trade was 1767-77; after this a decline set in which was greatly accelerated by the effects of the Napoleonic Wars. Newton Abbot was one of the ports from which ships sailed for Newfoundland. In those days ships were much smaller and could navigate the Teign as far as the Newton Quay. The

Trade and Communications

opportunity of earning some money by spending a summer in the North Atlantic attracted a good many men from Newton and the surrounding villages. These hopeful sailors congregated first at the Dartmouth Inn and later at the Newfoundland Hotel in East Street in the hope of being hired for a season's work.

The Dartmouth Inn still exists but the Newfoundland has been demolished; its name lives on in Newfoundland Way. The maritime associations of the pubs in East Street could be identified at the Jolly Sailor which was the previous name of the pub which is now the Jolly Abbot. There is also a Jolly Sailor pub in East Ogwell which indicates that the effects of the Newfoundland Trade were felt in the rural hinterland. The ships returned in the autumn with their cargo of dried cod. This was stored in depots in the town. There was one behind the Baptist Chapel in East Street and one in St John's Street, the latter street being named after the main port and capital of Newfoundland.

There was considerable economic spin-off from the Newfoundland Trade. Holbeam Mill supplied fish hooks and fishermen's knives, and boot and shoe makers in the town supplied waterproof fishermen's boots. Ridgways was one of these boot makers and **Rhodes** records that another bootmaker to the fishermen was called (appropriately) Crews and received large quantities of cod fish as payment. Perhaps the most famous landmark connected with the Newfoundland Trade is the Rope Walk in East Street, where rope was made. The Rope Walk which is signposted today once extended 140 yards to Hopkins Lane and there was a second rope walk which ran parallel to it. The existing walk was built in 1828 by Samuel Yeo. Samuel left it to his son Ephraim who built the tiny chapel called the East Street Room. There are two rooms, still to be seen, which contained the various materials used in the manufacture of rope, including coils of hemp imported from Bengal, and tallow and tar with which the coiled fibre was impregnated to make it waterproof and rot proof. There was a windlass worked by a horse to coil the fibre.

Ephraim Yeo invented a machine which added to the efficiency of the rope making process. He applied for a patent for this invention and a document, dated 1876, is in the care of Newton Abbot Town Council which bears the seal of Queen Victoria and reads as follows:

A Book of Newton Abbot

'Whereas Ephraim Yeo of Newton Abbot in the County of Devon, Rope Manufacturer, hath by his petition humbly represented unto us that he is in possession of an invention for improvements in the treating of yarns for packing purposes, which he believes will be of great public utility, the Queen has graciously granted to him the patent of this invention.'

Unfortunately, the patent document is no more precise than this regarding Ephraim Yeo's invention. In a Devon Directory of 1878, Ephraim Yeo is listed as a 'Patent Steam Engine Packing Manufacturer' so perhaps we can assume that by this time he had adapted the steam engine to the manufacture of rope and made his horse redundant.

The Rope Walk was inherited by Ephraim's nephew, John Brewer, and then by his son Charles. Charles Brewer was the last of the line to carry on the rope making business.

The Contribution of the Templers

James Templer was born into a poor family in Exeter in 1722. He ran away to sea and made a fortune in India. He returned and bought an estate near Newton Abbot which consisted of the infertile heathland of the Bovey Basin and the ruins of an old house known as Stoford Lodge. On a hilltop half a mile from these ruins and easily visible from the Bovey Road James Templer built Stover House of Haytor Granite. He also landscaped the grounds and excavated Stover Lake. James Templer died in 1782 and his estate was inherited by his son, also James. James Templer Junior continued his father's benevolent interest in the village of Teigngrace and endowed it with a new church, also built of Haytor Granite.

Towards the close of the eighteenth century, the trade in ball clay from the Bovey Basin was expanding steadily. This led to James Templer's decision to construct a canal from the head of the Whitelake Channel to Ventiford at Teigngrace. Templer's original scheme was to extend the canal to Jewsbridge near Heathfield, and from there to Bovey Tracey with a branch to Chudleigh. The Stover Canal, authorised and constructed in 1792, was the first canal to be dug in Devon since the Exeter Canal. However, Templer was financing the building of the canal through his

Trade and Communications

estate himself, and he obviously had second thoughts about his project when the canal had been excavated as far as Ventiford, for a terminal basin was dug there. This was followed by clay cellars and a yard for building barges suitable for the shipment of clay from Ventiford to Teignmouth.

Agricultural produce was transported along the canal and the Teign Estuary but there is no doubt that the transportation of clay from Ventiford Basin to the port of Teignmouth soon established itself as the most important traffic on the canal. Sometimes goods such as coal and manure were back-freighted from Teignmouth to the quays serving Newton or as far as Ventiford.

James Templer Junior left the Stover Estate, including the granite quarries at Haytor, to his son George. George Templer secured the contract to supply granite for the building of London Bridge and decided to construct a tramway between the quarries and Ventiford Basin as an efficient means of transporting the cut stone to the barges waiting on the Stover Canal. The single line of tramway was laid with rails made from granite, a readily available material which was cheaper and more reliable than the iron rails of the pre-railway age. This line fell more than 1,300 feet in seven miles and was opened in 1820. At this time, also, the Teign Estuary was improved and the New Quay at Teignmouth built between 1825 and 1827 by George Templer to facilitate, respectively, passage of waterborne traffic and the transfer of granite and clay from barge to ship.

The improved Teign navigation encouraged the growth of waterborne trade between points on the estuary. Market boats ran a regular service between Coombe Cellars and the Newton Quays. In 1827, when plans were invited by Richard Lane of Bradley Manor for new market buildings in Newton Abbot, one James Green submitted a plan which included the construction of a canal from a point on the Teign about half a mile below Newton Quay to a basin in the heart of the town. This canal would have had one tide lock at its entrance and would provide direct access to Newton Market by waterborne traffic, thus providing a more convenient means of trading than via the existing tidal quays.

The granite trade prospered but George Templer was a poor manager and fond of the arts and sports. He wrote poetry and founded the South Devon Hunt and the first cricket club in Devon. In 1829 he was forced to sell the estate, including the tramway and the canal, when both were very

71

profitable and all this property came into the ownership of the Duke of Somerset. George Templer must have experienced some temporary respite from his bad fortunes for he returned soon afterwards and built Sandford Orleigh, or rather rebuilt and added to the existing house. Sandford Orleigh is perhaps better known as the home of Sir Samuel Baker, who discovered one of the sources of the Nile and lived here from 1875-93. It is said that the view of the Teign Estuary which he enjoyed reminded him sufficiently of the great African river. His friend General Gordon spent the night at Sandford Orleigh before setting forth on his last fateful expedition to Khartoum. George Templer lived at Sandford Orleigh whilst employed as the Granite Company's chief agent in Devon. The company floundered, however, and the Secretary blamed George's incompetence. George Templer was killed in a hunting accident in 1843.

In 1850 the granite quarries and tramway were still busy and employed some one hundred men. By 1858, having supplied granite for the British Museum, the National Gallery and London Bridge, the trade was lost to Cornish coastal quarries where the stone could be more economically loaded directly into ships; instead of onto wagons, then barges, then ships. By this time the Haytor granite quarries and tramway were disused and deserted. The Stover Canal continued to be used for the transportation of clay but in 1862 it was sold to the Moretonhampstead and South Devon Railway who constructed a single-track, broad-gauge railway line from Newton Station alongside the Canal to Ventiford and from there along the track of the old granite tramway. Clay barges were towed down the canal in the 1920s and 30s by motor tug, this trade finally ceasing on the outbreak of World War II, when the little clay which was being dug was taken to Teignmouth by lorry.

There is little doubt that, without the contribution of the Templers, the South Devon ball clay trade would never have established itself so firmly. Their name is celebrated today in the creation, some fifteen years ago, of the Templer Way, an 18-mile route for walkers which once carried granite from Haytor and clay from Teigngrace to Teignmouth Docks, connecting Yarner Wood, Great Plantation, Stover, Jetty Marsh and along the south side of the Teign Estuary to Shaldon. It follows the northern boundary of built-up Newton Abbot (ref. Town Trail 3: Industrial Newton on page 151) and is waymarked in both directions by signs bearing the logo of a tramway wheel and barge tiller and rudder.

Trade and Communications

The Railway

By 1844 the Bristol and Exeter Railway was completed to Exeter and the South Devon Railway Company was formed with a view to extending the line to Plymouth. The Haldon Hills provided a major obstacle to the railway west of Exeter and the solution lay either in routing the line north of this elevated land via Ashburton or south via the coast to Newton Abbot. After a survey of road traffic using the two towns the southern route was decided upon. By the end of December, 1846, the line had reached Newton Abbot. The Queens Hotel opened in 1848 and Queen Street was developed to connect the newly arrived railway with the town centre.

At first the line was worked by steam locomotives but it did not prosper as anticipated and Isambard Kingdom Brunel, who was engineer on the line, persuaded the South Devon Railway Company that the line could be more profitably worked by the atmospheric method. This worked as follows: a continuous pipe was laid between the tracks in which a vacuum was produced by power supplied by engine houses built at the trackside at intervals of about three miles. Within the tube moved a piston which connected through a vertical driving rod with the train. The pipe therefore needed a longitudinal opening along its entire length which itself needed to be kept airtight. The solution lay in providing the opening in the tube with a flexible leather flap which was forced open by the driving rod and closed behind it as it moved forward.

The supposed advantages of this system were speed, silence, cleanliness and economy of running: one engine could propel many trains and need not pull heavy locomotives. Pipes were laid and pumping stations built between Exeter and Teignmouth and the atmospheric railway commenced operation in September, 1847. The system was extended to Newton Abbot in 1848. Engine houses were built to carry the atmospheric line as far as Totnes but this westerly section was never worked on the atmospheric principle.

Unfortunately for the South Devon Railway Company and for Brunel's reputation, this new-fangled railway was beset with problems from its delayed start to its abrupt end. The chief cause of trouble was the unreliability of an organic substance such as leather. The leather, although well greased, was subject to the extremes of the weather as well as to the

A Book of Newton Abbot

corroding effect of the sea air along the South Devon coast. The disintegration of the leather valve spoilt the vacuum and the atmospheric railway became less efficient. Brunel suggested that the entire valve flap be replaced by a new, improved version, but the directors of the South Devon overruled him and the atmospheric railway ceased working late in 1848. The conventional steam locomotives, which had so often come to the rescue of a stranded atmospheric train, now took over completely the running of the line. Not much remains to be seen of the atmospheric railway except some sections of pipe which are used as sewer pipes on the beaches near Teignmouth and Dawlish and an old engine house with Italianate tower at Starcross.

Rhodes records that 'it was only a year or two since that the old atmospheric tower at Newton Station was demolished', although the engine was resold to its makers in 1853. This means that the Newton tower stood for about fifty years, being demolished around 1900. There are two interesting pictures of the Newton tower in Charles Hadfield's book on atmospheric railways. Someone has suggested to me the quite plausible theory that the Italianate towers of Brunel's engine houses were a formative influence in the minds of the architects responsible for designing many of Newton Abbot's private houses and public buildings which sprang up during the building boom which followed the coming of the railway. One only has to look at some of the Victorian houses in Powderham Road and at the Alexandra Hall to see how central is the tower theme in these buildings.

The atmospheric left a more certain legacy and that is the steep inclines on the line between Newton Abbot and Plymouth. It was reckoned that trains propelled on the atmospheric principle could better cope with steep inclines than could trains propelled by steam locomotives. Before the advent of the more powerful diesel engines, many steam-powered trains needed two locomotives west of Newton Station, first to ascend the 1 in 37 Dainton incline and then others towards Plymouth. The South Devon Railway line reached Plymouth in 1848 and in the same year a branch line was opened from Newton Abbot to Torre. Pumping stations were built to power the atmospheric railway on this branch line but were never used.

The Moretonhampstead line from Newton Abbot was opened in 1866 and finally closed in 1959. The line still exists as far as Heathfield. This line enjoyed a brief renaissance during and immediately after World War II with the temporary flourishing of the Bovey coal industry. The Teign

74

The 'Newtonian' outside the Railway Station perparing to take travellers from the train off to the moors

Steam locomotive on tracks south of Forde Road

The former Newton Abbot Railway Station in the days of steam

Newton Abbot Railway Station, rebuilt 1926

Trade and Communications

Valley Railway from Heathfield to Ashton was opened in 1882 and to Exeter in 1903, when it formed a useful supplement to the main line along the coast when the latter was made impassable in stormy weather. This line died a gradual death from 1958 onwards.

Newton Abbot's railway station and works have been demolished and rebuilt more than once. The station was first rebuilt in 1861, before which there were two stations, one for the main line and one for the branch line to Torre. **Rhodes** refers to these two stations as 'nothing more than tumble-down sheds'. He explains that '...eventually a portion of one of the old sheds was accidentally knocked down, and it was then that the present station was erected, although it has since undergone various alterations, and extensions'. Newton Abbot Station was not named as such until 1877; before then it was simply 'Newton Station'. The station was entirely rebuilt in 1926; this is the station we see today.

In 1876 the Great Western Railway bought and worked the line of the South Devon Railway Company, impoverished as it was by the failure of the Atmospheric, an event which **Rhodes** reckons to have been 'one of the greatest benefits that could have fallen on Newton'. The GWR considerably extended the locomotive and carriage maintenance and repair works. The locomotive capacity was increased from 4 to 40 and a new set of carriage workshops introduced. **Rhodes** concludes that, 'the works are thus the centre of a big industry, and altogether there are nearly 600 employees'. Newton Abbot was the foremost railway repair works for the whole of the West Country. A town guide of the 1930s states that, at the time, the works employed 1,000 men. In 1960 the railway repair works were replaced by new facilities for the maintenance of diesel engines which were then being introduced into the Western Region of British Railways, as it had been since nationalisation in 1947. BR had employed 1,950 workers well into the 1950s, subsequent decades saw a dramatic decline – by 1990 fewer than 50 reported for duty. The locomotive repair works, where the finest maintenance work was achieved (and once broad gauge locomotives were built from scratch) are now a thing of the past.

Another feature which added to Newton Abbot's importance as a railway centre is the Hackney Goods Yard, built in 1911, whose extensive sidings at one time comprised the GWR's largest marshalling depot west of Bristol. Hackney Yard is now little used.

Until recently there were some interesting relics to be seen at Newton

Abbot Station to remind us of the past. In previous editions of this book, I noted that outside the station, in the corner of the garden wall to the left of the Railway Tavern public house, was a boundary stone of the old South Devon Railway which originally bore the initials 'SDR.' This has now been removed to make way for a drainage pipe from the house behind. High on the wall at the rear of the booking office hung a section of wrought iron, beautifully shaped, which once served as a grille in the old SDR booking office. This, I am informed, is 'in store'. On the staircase hung a clock which was presented to the GWR in 1926 by the town as a mark of thanks for the rebuilt station; this has now been replaced by a digital clock, though the shadow of the former incumbent can be seen. On the island platform itself stood 'Tiny', an original broad gauge locomotive. This was a reminder of Brunel's broad gauge railway line, the only one in the country which differed from the standard gauge used elsewhere. 'Tiny' worked the line for a number of years and was then employed as a stationary engine at Newton Abbot. She is the only surviving broad gauge locomotive still extant so is quite unique. She now resides at Buckfastleigh in the care of the South Devon Railway Trust. Remaining is a commemorative board listing those GWR employees who died in the two world wars. This can be seen on the footbridge to the island platform.

The many skilled men who had been employed at the locomotive and carriage repair works found new employment at Centrax, an engineering company specialising in power generation which relocated from London to Newton Abbot during the mid-1950s. A factory was built on woodland at the top of Shaldon Road and continues to be a major employer in the area.

2006 marked 200 years since the birth of Isambard Kingdom Brunel. Various events were held in Newton Abbot and beyond to mark 'Brunel 200' including special displays at the Town Museum , an 'Atmospheric Event' at Forde House and a Community Play specially written for the occasion by Tim Laycock and presented by Wren Music entitled 'A Wonderful Alteration' which was performed in Coombeshead Theatre over three days in May. The 'wonderful alteration' refers perhaps to many changes: from Brunel's broad gauge to standard gauge, from his atmospheric to steam locomotion but, perhaps most of all, the huge and lasting impact that the coming of the railway had on Newton Abbot.

5

The River Lemon

The most obvious intriguing point about the River Lemon must surely be its name which does not, disappointingly, bear any relation to the fruit. **Stirling** refers to the 'Lemmon' and informs us that the name is of Saxon origin and is taken from *Llam* – a stone, or its plural *Llaman* – stones, which, when associated with *Afon* – a river, signifies a stone, or stones in a river, to step over. In his book *Devon* (Bell, 1929), S E Winbolt notes that the river Lemon is a corruption of *Loman* which itself is an anglicised form of the Welsh word *Llyfnn* meaning smooth. But could the River Lemon be described as smooth? Gover's *Place Names of Devon* (Cambridge, 1931) gives the name Lemon as a derivative of a Celtic word meaning 'elm' and is variously referred to from early documents to more recent times as *Lime, Lymen, Limene, Leman* and *Lemman*. We can see from the above that there are many explanations of the origin of the name Lemon so I leave it to the reader to make his choice.

Before the coming of the railway in 1848 the main area of settlement in the twin towns of Newton Abbot and Newton Bushel was the area around East Street, Wolborough Street, Bank Street, Highweek Street, Back Road and Market Street. These are all thoroughfares in close proximity to the Lemon but far enough upstream for the river not to be subject to the influence of sea tides. The land below Hero Bridge (opposite the Tourist Information Centre) was marshy and liable to flooding. The existence of this area of marsh is evidenced by the naming of Marsh Road which runs along the banks of the Lemon. This immediate area (Osborne Park, Lemon Road, Gladstone Place, Albany Street) has always been liable to flooding and suffered especially badly in the years 1861, 1894, 1938

A Book of Newton Abbot

and 1979. During the 1938 flood Queen Street, Courtenay Street, Bank Street and Wolborough Street were also badly inundated.

A booklet was published following the 1894 flood entitled, *The Memorable Floods in and around Newton Abbot on November 14th, 1894*, in which the author, a Mr Chandler of the *Western Morning News*, gives a graphic and detailed description of the events which took place on that fateful day. In it he recalls the following:

> 'Comical scenes were witnessed as the ever-broadening stream came down the left hand side of Wolborough Street, and as the waters increased…completely submerging Bank Street. Ladies were imprisoned in shops by the sudden flood, and as some raised their skirts and waded through the water they were rewarded with rounds of laughter. Others, fearing to wet their shoes and feet, were borne across by stalwart men.'

Mr Chandler also relates: 'One of the most exciting events of the day' which was the rescue of a horse from the Lemon. A bolting horse reached the end of one of the courts in Wolborough Street and was swept away into the swirling torrents. It was carried underground through the tunnel which runs under Bank Street and Market Street to be thrust out into the open where the Lemon re-emerged at Sherborne Mill. The poor creature was eventually rescued at Lemon Road Bridge where some men pulled it out with the aid of a rope. The horse was badly bruised but still alive.

There are still areas of marsh to the north of Knowles Hill and Jetty Marsh Lane. These form the flood plain of the Teign rather than the Lemon, but one can get an idea of what 'lower' Newton Abbot must have looked like prior to the town's expansion towards the railway station. Newton Abbot Race Course was previously known as Teign Marshes. During a short period in most years the low lying fields north of Teign Bridge are submerged beneath the floodwaters of the Teign. An enormous lake of floodwater here provided a spectacular sight in February 1978 when the deep snow which had fallen everywhere in the catchment area of the Teign began to thaw.

Nevertheless, in general the Lemon and the Mill Leat which is fed by the Lemon have been friends to the town by providing fresh water and a source of energy to the various mills in Newton Abbot. It is illustrative of

Floods in Newton Abbot.
Above: A railway line washed away; note the power station in the background – the cooling tower was a dominant feature of the town until its demolition in 1974. Below: a flooded Marsh Road beside the River Lemon in 1979.

A Book of Newton Abbot

the use made of the Lemon to follow its course from the heights of Dartmoor down to its confluence with the Teign. The Lemon rises in the hills around Haytor and is fed by several springs in that area. Its route to the Teign Estuary is short and direct and the flow of its waters generally rapid. There are many mills along its banks, usually fed by leats channelled from the river.

Holbeam Mill was well known in the heyday of the Newfoundland trade for the manufacture of fish hooks and fishermen's knives, anchors, nails and other items of ironware. Holbeam had been an important mill for some time before because it is recorded that in 1648 Thomas Reynell had sold to John Reynell and Richard Brooking 'the manors of East Ogwell and West Ogwell with...the mills called Holbeam Mills'. I have found a reference to Holbeam being used as a grain mill and this was probably its original function.

With the demise of the Newfoundland trade in the second half of the nineteenth century, Holbeam Mill was sold to the Loder family who began manufacturing agricultural implements. An article in **TDA** 1934 records the following:

> 'There is a stall for the sale of these hand-wrought tools from Ogwell Edge-tool Mill in Newton Abbot Market, and though slightly more expensive, they long outlast any machine-made tools.'

It is clear from the article that the 'Ogwell Edge-tool Mill' referred to is, in fact, Holbeam Mill. Holbeam or Hobbin, as it is sometimes referred to, survives today, although no longer a working mill. It is now a private residence and the old mill machinery was transferred for preservation to the Science Museum in South Kensington, London.

Another famous mill on the Lemon was Ogwell Mill in Bradley Woods, a short way downstream from Chercombe Bridge, where the lane rises to Ogwell. This mill was reputed to be very old and was a renowned beauty spot and a favourite place for Newtonians and visitors to take a stroll. Ogwell had been a grain mill but had fallen into disrepair during the Second World War and was demolished soon after. Its exact position, as far as I can discern, was just about on the site of the present bungalow which stands at the corner of the Lemon and Ogwell Lane. Fragments of

Ogwell Mill: front view

Ogwell Mill: Rear view showing overshot water wheel

A Book of Newton Abbot

the original limestone walls of the old mill can still be seen, including what appears to be an arch over the leat which drove the waterwheel.

Many photographs and paintings of old Ogwell Mill exist and it seems surprising that so little is known about its origin and use. I have read of its supposed ecclesiastical origin but have found no evidence to support this claim. One or two elderly Newtonians I have spoken to can recall enjoying cream teas served at Ogwell Mill and I have also found a reference to a local craft which was practised there. This was the polishing of fossil corals found in the limestone quarries nearby which were fashioned into jewellery and ornaments, although I have yet to see a sample of this lost industry. A view of Ogwell Mill was used in the advertisements for the perfume called 'Bradley Woods Bouquet' which was manufactured and supplied by the former Bibbings the Chemist in Queen Street. This perfume is advertised in **Rhodes** and in many early editions of the Town Guide.

A little further downstream from Ogwell Mill there is a weir where water is diverted from the River Lemon to supply the Mill Leat which is here channelled alongside the footpath which leads to Bradley Manor. At the side of the little bridge over the leat near the main entrance to the Manor is a spring. This spring is a constant source of water and could be the reason why Bradley Manor is situated at this spot. Local tradition has it that the water from this spring possesses curative properties for the eyes and is sometimes referred to as a wishing well: to obtain your heart's desire you are supposed to drink the water then make your wish whilst turning around three times with eyes shut.

At this point let us leave the Lemon and follow the Mill Leat towards Bradley Mills at the head of Bradley Lane. Here its waters were used for many years in the wool and leather works, in the cleansing and dying processes and formerly as a source of energy. Water was pumped from the leat to a holding reservoir at the back of the mill on the slopes of Hangman's Hill. The leat emerges for a short stretch opposite the row of cottages in Bradley Lane and again disappears underground. One Newtonian has told me that he remembers a Mr Sampson, pork butcher in Highweek Street, who used to wash sausage skins in a trough at the side of his shop, the water being replenished from the Mill Leat. He can also recall water being pumped from the leat for cleaning the floor of the livestock markets after market day.

The River Lemon

Next use of the Mill Leat was made at Sherborne Mill, situated partly on the site where the cattle market now stands and bounded by Halcyon Road (formerly Mill Lane) and Market Street. The water wheel was adjacent to Halcyon Road. This mill was a flour mill and was also known as Coombe's Mill and Stockman's Mill, according to ownership. Sherborne Mill was demolished in the 1930s to make way for the new cattle market. At this latter site can be seen the old grey limestone Bark Mill. Here the waters of the leat provided the power to pulverise bark to extract tannin.

Let us now return to the Lemon outside Bradley Manor where we can follow its course along the boundary of Baker's Park towards the town. From Back Road we may cross the river using either of the two bridges, one being known as the Union Bridge. This bridge was built by public subscription in 1822. It may be so named because it made a physical union between the two communities, still politically separate in 1822, of Newton Abbot and Newton Bushel. Shortly past Union Bridge the Lemon flows underground, beneath buildings in Bank Street. The town map of 1843 shows the Lemon emerging for a short length on the far side of Bank Street and again at the bend where Market Street meets Sherborne Road. It was later enclosed as far as the present Hero Bridge, so named because a heroic feat was enacted here before the last war when a citizen of the town dived into the Lemon to rescue a drowning boy, or so the story goes. According to an article in **TDA** 1997, this river crossing was referred to as Lemon Bridge in 1621 when it was reported as being in need of repair. However, in 1882 the name Hero appeared for the first time but no explanation is offered.

The lower stretches of the Lemon through the town are tidal and it is when high tides combine with a swollen flow of water that floods occur. When I arrived in Newton Abbot in the exceptionally dry summer of 1976 I remember the Lemon as a mere trickle of water struggling seaward over the paved river bed through the town.

In February 1978, when the snows that fell during the Great Blizzard began to thaw the waters increased tremendously in volume and velocity. I remember gazing at the river from Union Bridge and wondering at the sheer speed of the flow. The river was near to bursting its banks for several days. Council workmen sandbagged houses and shops in the danger area and kept a watchful eye on water levels but the thaw was not as rapid as it could have been and disaster was averted.

In December 1979 the river burst its banks and flooded lower Newton Abbot to a depth of several feet, causing much damage and misery. 'DELUGE OF DISASTER' was the headline in the *Mid-Devon Advertiser*. Residents of houses in the little terraced streets flanking the Lemon had to be evacuated on the night of the 27th December. At Newton Abbot Library we realised what was likely to be in store for us and made sure no books were left stacked on the ground floor. Just as well as next morning it was clear that we had suffered a 'flash flood'; the parquet flooring was obscured beneath a deposit of silt with a rippled surface like you would see on a beach at low tide!

Almost all the properties in the main shopping streets, including the then just completed Market Walk, were under two to three feet of water in the early hours of Friday morning. What made matters far worse was the fact that on Thursday, the day after Boxing Day, a good many of the shops were shut and so unattended. However, the town soon got back to normal: there were some bargains to be had among 'Flood Damaged Stock' and 1980 saw more painting and refitting of shops in Newton Abbot than for many a year, as owners received their insurance claims.

The much debated Flood Prevention Scheme became a reality in 1981 when the Lemon was dammed upstream at Holbeam in 1982. This long overdue measure was completed in 1982 by the South-West Water Authority at a cost of £628,000. The dam is able to hold back some 900 million gallons and can cope with a depth of up to 20 feet of water in a 34 acre storage area. Its first major test occurred in December 1989 when torrential rain led to the accumulation of 22 million gallons and again in February of the following year with 40 million gallons. On these occasions the Holbeam Dam, together with the strengthening and raising of the river banks below Bradley Mill, undoubtedly saved Newton Abbot from flooding.

I am no fisherman and leave it to those who are to confirm the veracity of this little rhyme, often quoted in old guide books on Newton Abbot:

'The Teign for Salmon, the Dart for Peel,
Fort Leat for Trout and the Lemon for Eel.'

6

John Lethbridge: Famous Son

If Newton Abbot has a famous son it must surely be John Lethbridge. Lethbridge was a wool merchant and lived at 83, Wolborough Street. By the age of forty he had seven children, was in some financial difficulties and sought a way of improving his fortunes. To this end Lethbridge perfected a diving machine which would allow him to submerge himself at the bottom of the sea, without contact of air, for long enough to salvage valuables from wrecks.

His first experiments were carried out in 1715 in his orchard. Here he dug a pond in which he submerged himself in a sealed barrel and remained underwater for half-an-hour. This having been successful, he forwarded detailed plans for the construction of a diving engine to a cooper in London.

There was some correspondence in *Gentlemen's Magazine* in 1749 in which one Samuel Ley describes a diving boat constructed by Mr Symons, a house carpenter of Harberton, who had demonstrated his invention by submerging himself in the River Dart. Samuel Ley also states that the same man 'invented the famous diving engine for taking up of wrecks'. Some two months later, *Gentlemen's Magazine* published a letter from John Lethbridge in which he himself claims to be the inventor of the first diving machine to function without communication of air and proceeds to give a detailed description of his invention, as follows:

> 'It is made of wainscot perfectly round, about six feet in length, about two feet and a half diameter at the head, and about eighteen inches diameter at the foot, and contains about thirty gallons; it is hoop'd with iron hoops without and within to

A Book of Newton Abbot

guard against pressure. There are two holes for the arms, and a glass about four inches diameter, and an inch and a quarter thick to look thro', which is fixed in the bottom part, so as to be in a direct line with the eye, two air-holes upon the upper part, into one of which air is conveyed by a pair of bellows, both which are stopt with plugs immediately before going down to the bottom. At the foot part there's a hole to let out water. Sometimes there's a large rope fixed to the back or upper part, by which it's let down, and there's a little line called the signal line, by which the people above are directed what to do, and under is fix'd a piece of timber as a guard for the glass. I go in with my feet foremost, and when my arms are got thro' the holes, then the head is put on, which is fastened with screws. It requires 500 weight to sink it, and take but 15 pound weight from it and it will buoy upon the surface of the water. I lie straight upon my breast all the time I am in the engine, which hath many times been more than six hours, being frequently refreshed upon the surface by a pair of bellows. I can move it about 12 foot square at the bottom, where I have stayed many times 34 minutes. I have been ten fathoms deep many a hundred times, and have been 12 fathom, but with great difficulty.'

One of his most famous salvage operations was on the Dutch merchant ship, the *Slot ter Hooge*, which had sunk off Madeira in 1724 with over three tons of silver aboard. A silver tankard existed which bore engravings showing John Lethbridge's diving machine being hoisted up or down from a boat and a map of Porto Santo (Madeira) on which is marked the location of the wrecked ship. Robert Stenuit, the Belgian diver, researched the records concerning the treasure on board when the ship sank and that recovered by Lethbridge and reckoned there must be a worthwhile amount still at the bottom of the sea.

In 1974 Stenuit led an expedition to locate the rest of the treasure. During his endeavour, he developed a keen interest in John Lethbridge, the man who had dived on this same wreck in his contraption made of wood, iron and leather some two and a half centuries earlier. Stenuit had a replica of Lethbridge's diving machine constructed and tested to his

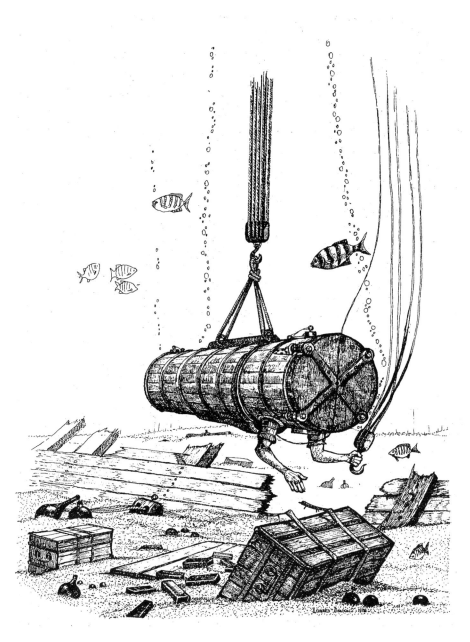

Impression of John Lethbridge salvaging treasure in his diving machine

A Book of Newton Abbot

satisfaction, but only after a great deal of experimentation with the leather arm sockets, details of which Lethbridge had strategically omitted from his description quoted above. The Belgian diver's exploration of the *Slot ter Hooge* and John Lethbridge's diving machine were made into a television programme by the BBC which was first broadcast in 1977.

A **TDA** article in 1880 describes an inscribed board dated 1736 at the house of Lethbridge's grandson. It states the following:

> 'John Lethbridge, by the blessing of God, has dived on the wrecks of four English Men-of-war, one English East Indiaman, two Dutch East Indiamen, two Spanish galleons, and two London galleys, all lost in the space of twenty years; on many of them with good success, but he has been very near to drowning in the engine five times.'

John Lethbridge made his fortune and purchased the Odicknoll Estate in Kingskerswell. Nevertheless, he continued his preoccupation with diving on wrecks and in 1757, at the age of eighty one, he had written to the English East India Company asking for the contract to dive on a ship which had recently sunk. Needless to say he did not get the contract. He died two years later. He was buried at Wolborough Church. A note in the parish register records the following:

> 'December 11th, 1759. Buried Mr John Lethbridge, inventor of a most famous diving-engine, by which he recovered from the bottom of the sea, in different parts of the globe, almost £100,000 for the English and Dutch merchants which had been lost by shipwreck.'

7
Views of Newton Abbot through the Twentieth Century

Drumclock Corner, prior to erection of Lloyd's Bank building

Junction of Highweek Street and Old Exeter Road just prior to demolition of the properties between

Halcyon Road, prior to widening, a somewhat quieter thoroughfare

View along lane at rear of Foss's Corner in 1937 towards the Golden Lion Inn. Bills posted on the wall include one advertising a production of 'Lovers Leap' and The Pavilion, Torquay; others urge Newtonians to 'Join the Modern Army' or the TUC with the slogan 'It Pays to Organise'.

View down Bank Street from the Library, showing buildings on Foss's Corner before their demolition

Market Street from Bank Street, before the erection of the Liberal Club

Bank Street from the Globe Hotel (now part of Austin's store)

Courtenay Street from the Globe Hotel, showing former Wesleyan Methodist Church in middle distance

View along busy Queen Street during the 1950s. The Commercial Hotel is still intact on the left corner, having not yet been demolished to make way for the Pearl Assurance building.

Left: View along The Avenue – note the cooling tower of the power station peeking above the rooftops

Below: Looking down Queen Street from the same spot, the spire of the former Congregational Church in the distance

The oak tree which formerly stood on the site of the War Memorial. Above: from junction of St. Paul's Road with Queen Street; Right: from The Avenue

The oak tree felled to make way for the war memorial (unveiled 1922) showing the Bible Christian Jubilee Chapel and Minister's residence in background

Queen Street with Imperial Electric Theatre

View along Torquay Road – note signpost indicating Prospect Chapel below to left

East Street, many of whose buildings still stand

Shapley Court, a typical Wolborough Street court, pictured in 1962, in the area now occupied by Newfoundland Way and the car park

Coombeshead Road from Ashburton Road, before the schools and many houses were erected

Pit Hill Road leading to Highweek Village, before modern development

Junction of Shaldon and St Marychurch Roads, prior to the development of the Milber-Buckland area

Decoy Road

Decoy, Newton Abbot, with view towards Wolborough Hill

8

Newton Abbot seen in old maps

The Town Survey of 1843

The main shopping streets of the town today are Courtenay and Queen Streets. Both these streets have a decidedly Victorian appearance and, in fact, barely existed until the coming of the railway. Courtenay Street was cut to connect the centre of Newton Abbot with the new road to Kingsteignton which was begun in 1836. The town survey of 1843 shows Queen Street as a mere lane or footpath leading off Courtenay Street in an easterly direction; the only buildings in Courtenay Street were the Globe Hotel, built by the Earl of Devon in 1842 as a coaching and posting house and then known as the Devon Arms, and a few properties at the St Leonard's Tower end of the street. Murray's *Handbook for Devon and Cornwall*, published in 1859, describes the Globe Inn, as it was known by then, as 'good and cheap'.

All the shops and inns and houses at this time were situated in Wolborough, East, Bank and Highweek Streets. The broad part of Wolborough Street from St Leonard's Tower (see frontispiece illustration) towards the corner of Newfoundland Way was known as High Street prior to 1826, the year in which the market was moved from here to its new site in Market Street. There were many inns and public houses in this area. The Ship Inn still exists but the 1843 Survey shows the Bear Inn right next door and further down towards the new St Leonard's Chapel were the Half Moon, the Compass Inn (latterly known as the Royal Oak) and the Turk's Head. The Turk's Head is now the Raj Belash Restaurant. Also

103

in High Street on this side was the Post Office.

Many old properties on this south side of what is now Wolborough Street have been demolished and Newfoundland Way and the large car park behind have been laid out on the cleared land. Wolborough Street led to the main road, now marked 'Old Totnes Road', which forked on the rise of Abbotskerswell Hill. The left fork led via Marldon to Kingswear for Dartmouth and the right fork via Totnes and Modbury to Plymouth.

Back Road connects Highweek Street with Wolborough Street and once formed a short link in the road from Exeter via Teignbridge to Dartmouth; it led this important route to a fording place across the River Lemon. In 1822 the Union Bridge was built by public subscription to span the Lemon at this point, although Back Road was no longer an important thoroughfare at that time, having been superseded by Bridge Street, formerly North Street (before 1800 when the bridge was built), and now Bank Street. Union Bridge survives today, with its commemorative tablet and with another stone footbridge standing beside it.

The Town Survey of 1843, entitled Plan of Two Towns of Newton, shows Bearne's Lane leading off Bridge Street towards Bearne's Timber Yard. The Golden Lion was there and so too was the London Hotel, situated on the corner opposite the Library, now part of the ASDA Superstore. Lane's Buildings in Market Street were named after Rev Richard Lane of Bradley Manor who built them in 1825, at the same time as the new market. **Stirling** describes Lane's Buildings as 'genteel looking houses with ornamental flowerpots in front and enclosed from the street by palisades'. They can be seen today set back from the road and lying between the Liberal Club and Rendells.

If we continue up Bridge Street past the junctions with Market Street and Back Road we find that the Newton Bank stood opposite the latter. The Newton Bank was founded in 1817, was absorbed by the Capital and Counties Bank in 1891 which in turn was absorbed by Lloyds Bank. Mr Pinsent's Minerva House (still there) stood with its famed garden stretching alongside the tree-lined mill leat towards Stockman's Mill. The Swan Inn was then next door to the Commercial Inn; the latter was demolished to make way for the Highweek Street entrance to the new cattle market in 1938. Further up Highweek Street Samuel Branscombe's Tannery stood on the left at the entrance to Bradley Lane, with Vicary's Works behind. Continuing up Highweek Street, across the main artery of

Newton Abbot see in Old Maps

the mill leat, which ran by the side of Palk and Pinsent's Brewery. Past St Mary's Chapel on the right and the Seven Stars Inn (see front cover picture) on the left, there was a fork in the road (see upper picture page 92), a feature which existed until the new Exeter Road was built.

The left fork led past scattered cottages to the Ashburton Road while the right fork led to what is marked on the 1843 map as the 'Old Road to Exeter', via Teign Bridge. The fork in the road can be traced today in Highweek and Old Exeter Roads. Not far along the Exeter Road was the driveway to Abbotsbury House; this still exists as a footpath and connects Exeter Road with Waverley Road. Abbotsbury House stood on Treacle Hill and at that time was the property of one William Francis D'Arcy Esq., but later in the nineteenth century was acquired by the Fisher family. The origin of the name Fisher Road in Abbotsbury is thus obvious. Less so is the unusual naming of Halcyon Road. It has been suggested to me that Mr Fisher was responsible for its extension towards Kingsteignton Road and decided on Halcyon Road because that is the term used for the male king*fisher* bird. The 1843 Survey gives Halcyon Road, or at least the Highweek Street end which existed in those days, as Mill Lane: it connected Bradley Lane with Stockman's Mill. **Stirling** lists one L. Stockman of Newton Bushel as a baker and miller so we can be certain that the mill at this time was used for milling flour.

East Street was at least as important a street before the advent of the railway as Wolborough Street. **Stirling** tells us that 'the ancient name of this street was Forde Street, afterwards Keyberry Street, and about the commencement of the eighteenth century it began to receive the appellation of East Street, on account of its direction'. This is rather confusing because Keyberry Mill is reputed to date back to Saxon times whilst the 'hamlets of Forde' are first mentioned in 1543.

The Court House was situated in East Street at the junction with Wolborough Street and is now occupied by the Tower Restaurant, formerly the Vecchia Roma Restaurant and 'Ye Olde Bunne Shoppe' (see frontispiece illustration) before that. Past here are the Union Inn and the White Hart, both of which still exist. Next to the White Hart was the Register Office. The Jolly Sailor (now the Jolly Abbot) was opposite the Newfoundland Inn (now demolished). The Dartmouth Inn was followed by the Town Arms (now the Greene Man); the Olde Cider Bar is not indicated (so perhaps not so old!). Opposite the Union Workhouse (now the Geriatric

A Book of Newton Abbot

Unit of Newton Abbot Hospital) was a property belonging to Samuel Yeo, including a 'Ropery', i.e. the Rope Walk. Properties on the opposite side of East Street included the Baptist Church (now the Spiritualist Church) and, way past the Union Workhouse and just outside the Toll Gate, the Widows' Almshouses of Lady Lucy Reynell, later rebuilt towards St Leonard's Tower.

The Ordnance Survey of 1888

The South Devon Railway reached Newton Abbot in 1848 and the changes that followed in its wake are evident in the Ordnance Survey maps drawn some forty years later. Means of access had to be constructed to link the centre of town with the Railway Station at the head of the Teign Estuary. This is how Queen Street (formerly Station Road) was built, but without so many shops as there are at present. Much of the land between the Station and the town belonged to the Earl of Devon; in 1854 Courtenay Park was laid out together with building sites along the newly created streets and squares.

Wolborough Local Board was formed in 1864 and the advent of local government certainly favoured the development of the Newton Abbot side of town. The Board was primarily concerned to improve the sanitary arrangements which in turn made possible the planned development of large areas, and to acquire the markets in order to rebuild them. **Rhodes** gives the following dates of construction: Fairfield Terrace between 1853-54, St Leonard's Road begun about 1860-61, Tudor Road (named after Rev Tudor, sometime Rector of Wolborough in 1866 and Union Street, the last important thoroughfare to be opened, in 1885.

Certainly by 1888 the appearance of the town was quite different. The railway changed Newton from being just a market town with its associated trades based on leather and wool to become, in addition, a base for industry. As well as the extensive Great Western Railway Works, many industries set up in close proximity to the Station. The grain and cider depot and maltings were constructed in Teign Road adjacent to railway sidings. Nearby, between the River Lemon and Osborne Park and including the site cleared by the demolition of Power Station in 1972 was a timber yard with tramways – the 'West of England Saw Mills'. An Iron and Brass

Newton Abbot see in Old Maps

Foundry and engineering works are also indicated; these are the premises of H. Beare and Sons which was founded in Liverton in the mid-nineteenth century and moved to Newton Abbot in 1884. Beare's traditionally specialised in making machinery for local industries such as clay and cider.

Workers flocked into Newton to man these new industries and the town's population increased tremendously during these years: from 1,623 in 1801 when the first census was taken, it grew to 5,998 in 1861 and to 12,518 in 1901. The terraced streets were built to house the workers whilst many attractive villas were built on the elevated ground of Wolborough and Knowles Hills, as well as on the Devon Estate around Courtenay Park and Devon Square, for the wealthier residents engaged in commerce and the professions, and advantage of its healthy climate and convenient location on the main railway line.

The first buildings to be erected in Queen Street were the terrace of cottages next to the Railway Station. This terrace was flanked by the Railway Hotel (now Railway Tavern) and the London Inn, which no longer exists. Opposite these stood the Queen's Hotel which still serves the town. A large oak tree stood where the memorial stands at the foot of St Paul's Road (see illustrations page 91) and opposite this at the centre of the junction there was a drinking fountain and horse trough. One old Newtonian I spoke to remembers the Devon and Courtenay's carts from Decoy Pit stopping here on their way to the Newton Quays to allow the horses to refresh themselves. The Masonic Hall in Devon Square was built in 1867. The Avenue was built by 1888 but was originally known as Lower St Paul's Road. On the corner opposite the present Methodist Church were houses with front gardens. This pleasant frontage was later despoiled by the erection of shop fronts and a car showroom.

Looking along Osborne Street from The Avenue, there stood a terrace of cottages on the right hand side and overlooking Osborne Park; yet another car park is to be found here today. The stone cottages on the left side of Salisbury Road as seen from Osborne Street are given on the 1888 map as 'Foundry Cottages' and no doubt housed workers from the nearby foundry.

Number 49 Queen Street was the Newton Club for Gentlemen, number 45 the Courtenay Arms (still there) and number 23 the Temperance Hall. Behind Queen Street there was a long terrace of cottages in Victoria Place. The Commercial Hotel (see iluustration page 95) stood at the junction of

107

Queen Street and Kingsteignton Road but has since been replaced by the Pearl Assurance Building. In Courtenay Street was to be found the Prince of Wales public house (now vanished) and, further along on the same side, the Town Hall and the Courtenay Street Hall, both demolished in 1977 to make way for Market Walk, and on the corner the Globe Hotel.

Highweek Street in 1888 would have been reasonably familiar to someone who had not visited the town since the 1843 survey. The River Lemon between Foss's Island (where several shops had replaced the London Hotel – now a vacant lot) and the Bradley Inn, had been covered so that it was no longer visible at the surface between Back Road and the far side of the new market buildings. Thus the 'bridge' of Bridge Street was no longer to be seen and Bridge Street became known as Bank Street, after the Newton Bank further up towards Highweek Street. The Swan Inn and Commercial Inn (sometimes referred to as the Old Commercial, to distinguish it from the new hotel in Queen Street) led to Palk and Pinsent's Brewery, given on the 1888 map as the Newton Brewery, in distinction to the brewery beside the Lemon in Back Road which is shown as 'Old Brewery', possibly no longer functioning as such. Another interesting feature on the 1888 map is Polyblank's Iron and Brass Foundry, situated at the southern end of Polyblank Road and burnt down some years later.

If we return to Market Street we find that the corner where the Library and Adult Education Centre are now situated was known as Harvey's Corner because of the shop of that name to be found there. The Market House Inn was around the corner then as today, as well as the Bradley Inn. The Post Office was opposite the Bradley. Sherborne Corn Mill was still going strong, opposite the recently built Alexandra Hall and market buildings. East Street featured an Armoury behind the former Newfoundland Inn and yet another pub – the Sun Inn, stood opposite the Union Inn. Number 36 East Street accommodated a Cottage Hospital and Dispensary. It is interesting to find **Rhodes** passing an uncharacteristically sorrowful comment on the many new houses provided for working people up until the turn of the century as follows:

> 'It is to be regretted that some of the new districts were not more judiciously laid out. For instance, the bye-laws might have been amended, so as to provide roads of greater width, and for more air space for each house.'

Newton Abbot see in Old Maps

The main changes which took place in the town between the surveys of 1843 and 1888 can be summed up as follows: the arrival of the railway, the growth of new industry largely dependent on the railway, the consequent increase in population and the development of housing and shopping facilities, and the renewal and expansion of the market.

1907 and after

The map reproduced on the following two pages first appeared in a handbook on Newton Abbot published in 1907. It shows the town which was familiar to those Newtonians who were children before the First World War. The Edwardian expansion of residential building was underway in the Abbotsbury area, in Coronation Road (named after the Coronation of Edward VII in 1901) and in the Decoy area. Many of the landmarks given still exist, although many buildings have changed their functions since 1907. Some of the properties in the town centre and along the main thoroughfares have been demolished and rebuilt but perhaps the most obvious change is the tremendous growth of the town in terms of housing accommodation and industrial building.

The 1907 map was drawn before the development of Buckland, Milber Down, Newtake and Aller Brake which began before World War II. A map dated 1927 shows only Addison Road, Limetree Walk and Pinewood Road on the Milber side; a map of 1948 shows the beginnings of Queensway, Buckland Brake and Oakland Road, although a few houses had been erected in this last road just prior to the Second World War. Milber was a wooded area and Milber Pine Woods were once far more extensive than they are now; Aller Brake also extended from the edge of the pine woods right down to Aller Village.

The Broadlands Estate was built on land bounded by Ashburton Road, Highweek Road and the mills and tanneries in Bradley Lane. It was named after Broadlands House, a former home of the Vicary family and reached from the Ashburton Road, was formerly an old people's home and is currently a Sixth Form Centre for Knowles Hill and Coombeshead Schools. Highweek was a community still distinct from Newton Abbot, or Newton Bushel. The slope of Highweek Hill north of the Ashburton Road is now covered with houses, as is the Bradley Barton and Bradley Valley

109

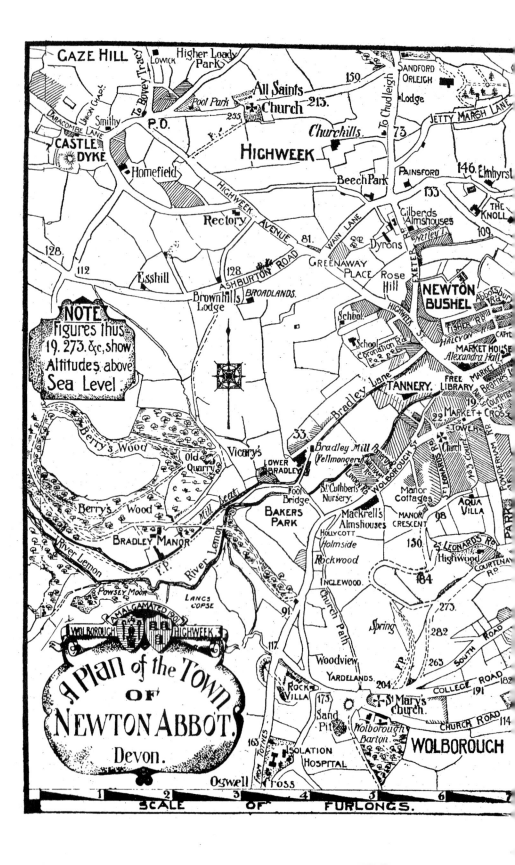

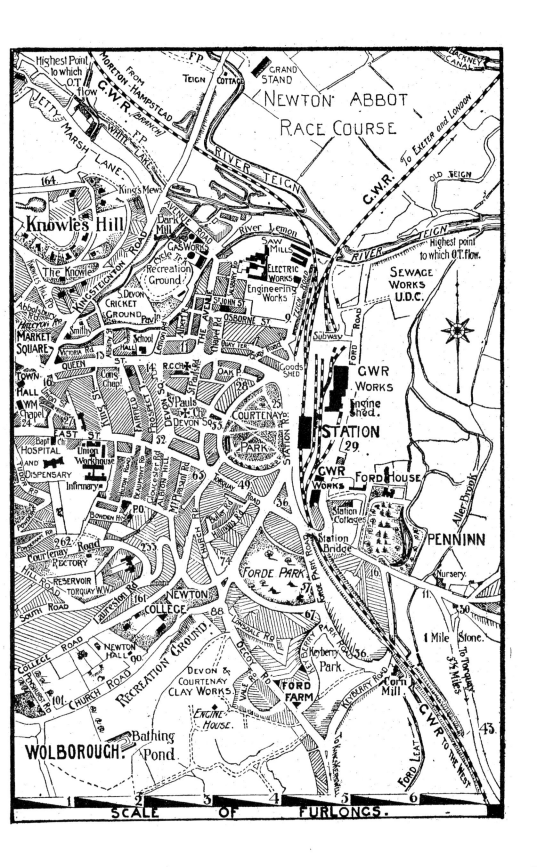

A Book of Newton Abbot

areas on the south side. Private houses have been built at Churchills, another former home of the Vicary family.

Since the last war new industrial development has been centred on the old industrial area at Bradley Lane, at the Centrax factory at the top of Buckland and in the new industrial estates in Brunel Road and at Decoy. Before the last war industrial activity was centred around the Railway Station and the wool and leather works. It is perhaps difficult to see which direction Newton Abbot is taking today, with the influx of retired people to South Devon, but traditionally it has been a working town with industrial and commercial activity centred on the market, on wool and leather, on the railway and, since the decline of the railway works, on engineering. This fact was recognised as an attraction in the past as this extract from a town guide of the 1930s makes plain:

'Newton is in the very forefront of South Devon's industrial towns, and, therefore, has a large working-class population, which ensures prices being kept reasonably low, as is not always the case in purely residential towns.'

During the present century, Newton Abbot's population has increased from 12,518 in 1901 to 18,290 in 1971, and around 25,000 in 2001.

9

Church and Chapel

Wolborough and Highweek Parish Churches stand opposite each other on hills between which run the River Lemon and the parish boundary. Both churches served ancient settlements which grew up nearby.

Highweek Parish

All Saints Church, Highweek, was built by Richard Yarde of Bradley Manor and was consecrated by Bishop Lacy of Exeter in 1428 in honour of All Saints. All Saints was a festival which had been celebrated in Newton Bushel since 1309. Before All Saints was built there stood on this site a chapel-of-Ease to St Michael's Church, Kingsteignton, which dated back at least to the thirteenth century when it is mentioned in documents. Originally, therefore, Highweek was included in the Parish of Kingsteignton.

There was no burial ground at Highweek and the dead had to be carried, via the Church Path, to the mother church in Kingsteignton. Highweek parishioners appealed to the Pope, pointing out the distance to Kingsteignton Church, the bad state of the roads and the regular flooding of much of the land to be traversed. Highweek Church, although granted the right of sepulture, remained a chapel-of-ease to Kingsteignton and retained this status until 1864 when it separated from Kingsteignton and became a parish in its own right.

All Saints Church in Highweek has a charming and lovingly cared for interior. In the north Bradley Aisle can be seen memorial tablets and vaults in which members of the Yarde family are buried.

The origin of St. Mary's Chapel-of-Ease in Highweek Street is clouded in uncertainty. Accounts vary but the most likely is that its origin was

A Book of Newton Abbot

contemporary with that of Bradley Manor, i.e. sometime in the thirteenth century, and that in 1448 Richard Yarde added a large chantry chapel to the original church. It is likely that its site is a very ancient one, standing as it does beside a spring on the old Exeter-Dartmouth Road. One can easily imagine the early missionaries preaching here and using the spring water to baptise those converted to Christianity. Most accounts of St. Mary's agree that it had a beautiful interior which was spoilt in 1826 when the arcade was destroyed by four arches being taken down and three galleries added. Rev Harris, first Rector of Highweek, spent £1,200 on renovating the interior of the chapel to repair the damage done in 1826. The lofty tower has two sculptured niches over its entrance which once contained statues; the bell bears the inscription: 'Jacob Nickell and William Pethybridge – Churchwardens. Mordecai Coakey cast me in Totnes 1686.'

Opposite St. Mary's Chapel stood the 'Seven Stars' pub (see front cover picture) which closed in 1978 and was demolished two years later. There is no doubt that this pub had an ancient origin. It was one of many inns found near churches which was dedicated to the Virgin Mary, who traditionally wore seven stars on her celestial crown. I have been told that its pre-Reformation name was 'Seven Stars of Our Lady'. Further down Highweek Street opposite the entrance to the Cattle Market was the Old Priest's House, demolished in 1976. In 1845 two chandeliers were removed from St. Mary's Chapel and a bill was circulated offering a reward to anyone giving information leading to their recovery. This theft turned out to be the work of members of Teignbridge Cricket Club who had hung them in Teigngrace Pavilion where a Jubilee Ball was being held.

In 1893 a Highweek parishioner, Miss Elizabeth Taylor, paid for the building of a Church Institute 'as a reading, lecture and class room, and meetings for the spiritual and social welfare of the parishioners.' A stone in the wall of this edifice commemorates 'Church Institute, 1897'. The new St. Mary's in Abbotsbury, on the site of Abbotsbury House on Treacle Hill, was built to cope with a growing congregation. This church was opened in 1906 and St. Mary's Chapel in Highweek Street became redundant and remained empty and unused for some twenty years. In the 1920s the Council leased the Alexandra Hall to a cinema company and the Rector of Highweek suggested that old St. Mary's Chapel be converted into a hall, leaving a tiny chapel under the tower to be used for occasional special services. The Newton Abbot Repertory Company opened St.

Church and Chapel

Mary's Hall in 1927 with a production of two one-act plays and continued to perform there for forty years. The Hall was also used by the Newton Abbot Society for the Arts for many musical performances. St. Mary's Hall is no longer used, but is superseded by facilities at the Community Centre in Kingsteignton Road and at the Dyrons Complex.

St. Mary's Chapel/Hall and Highweek Church School were renovated and converted to living accommodation in the 1980s, their grey limestone walls standing close by busy Highweek Street. The imposing edifice of St. Mary's Church in Abbotsbury seems large in relation to its present congregation as well as to the Edwardian brick-built houses which stand in orderly rows on all sides.

Wolborough Parish

The Parish Church of Wolborough is also dedicated to St. Mary and the present structure dates from the fifteenth century, although its Norman font and west tower indicate an origin in earlier times. It is said that St. Mary's in Wolborough was the last church in Devon in which Mass was celebrated at the time of the Reformation. King Charles I attended Divine Service here when he was staying at Forde House in 1625.

St. Mary's in Wolborough has a beautiful and interesting interior. John Lethbridge, the inventor of the diving machine, is buried in the extensive graveyard outside the Church and his name is mentioned on two boards in the entrance as follows: 'This Church was beautifyed in the year 1710 by the Feoffees – John Lethbridge, Will. Jones, Churchwardens.' A second board lists the Feoffees and includes the name of John Lethbridge.

The church is built in the perpendicular style and has a spacious feel. The magnificent brass eagle used as a lectern was found on Bovey Heath where, according to **Rhodes**, it was probably buried at the time of the Great Rebellion. A hagioscope, or squint, was discovered and reopened in 1881 during work to install an organ chamber and vestry, and this helps people sitting in the pews here to see the altar. The sanctuary itself contains a magnificent monument to the Reynell family. Sir Richard Reynell is depicted in armour with his wife, Lady Lucy, lying beside him. Below them lies their daughter Jane and their infant grandson. There is an epitaph full of praise for Sir Richard and a record of Lady Lucy's death,

A Book of Newton Abbot

the first letters of the last ten lines of which spell LUCY REYNEL.

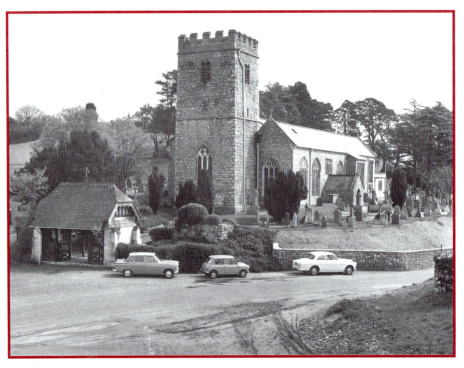

St. Mary's, Wolborough, pictured in about 1964

St. Mary's Church on Wolborough Hill is connected to St. Leonard's Chapel-of-Ease, of which the tower now only remains, by the Church Path. The age of the original St. Leonard's is difficult to ascertain although the fact that the church is dedicated to St. Leonard, the Patron Saint of prisoners, indicates that it may date back to the time of the Crusades when many a Crusader was captured and imprisoned abroad. The first mention of St. Leonard's is in a document dated 1350, although it seems likely to have had its beginnings in the early thirteenth century. The right to hold a market in the expanding community on the south bank of the Lemon was granted to the Abbots of Torre in 1220 and it seems reasonable to assume that a church was built here to cater for the spiritual needs of an expanding community.

Stirling, writing shortly before the nave of St. Leonard's was demolished in 1836 in a bid to ease traffic congestion in Wolborough Street, describes the chapel as follows:

Church and Chapel

'This gothic remnant of antiquity, stands in the centre of the street, at the cross. It is of but small dimensions, being only 55 feet long, by 20 broad, and consist of a lofty nave; at the west end of which, rises a square embattled tower to the height of 60 feet. The interior displays nothing calculated to challenge attention, if the old oak seats, east of the font, are excepted, all of which, bear the features of extreme old age.... In the tower are six bells and an excellent clock. Here are solemnised, the sacrament of Baptism, and the institution of marriage, the other clerical duties are discharged at Wolborough, which is the parish church.'

The nave was, in fact, capable of seating 191 people and had three large windows on either side. There was a door on the south side of the church which formed a private entrance to the Ralegh pew. Members of this distinguished Devon family lived in a house on the site of the present Union Inn in East Street.

St Leonard's Tower from Wolborough Street pictured in the early 1960s. Note the Odeon Cinema on left; this opened in 1936 and closed in 1972.

The later St. Leonard's Church further along Wolborough Street was built in 1836 to replace the old St. Leonard's. This building no longer serves as place of worship but became St Leonard's Antiques and Craft Centre at the turn of the century. Although the old tower was restored in 1874, in 1897 there was a move to demolish the tower too. There was much opposition to this and the Society for the Protection of Ancient Buildings conducted a postcard poll in Newton Abbot which produced an overwhelming majority of 90% of townspeople in favour of keeping the tower. This process of partial demolition and rebuilding of St. Leonard's has resulted in the curious phenomenon of a street which contains a tower without a church and a church without a tower. The bells of St. Leonard's Tower ceased to be used before World War II but in 1969 the Tower and its bells were restored. The Tower stands today at the commercial heart of Newton Abbot but remembering nobler times: the proclamation of Prince William in 1688 and of all monarchs since.

But let us return to the mother church of St. Mary's in Wolborough. A board on the south wall gives us a brief history of the Parish of Wolborough as follows:

> 'William Brewer founded the Abbey of Torre in 1196 and presented the Manor and Advowson of Wolborough to the Abbot as part of the endowment. The Abbots were rectors of Wolborough until 1539 and the Church was served by the Canons of Torre. In 1539 the Abbey was dissolved and its endowments sold. After several changes the Manor and Advowson passed into the hands of the Courtenays when Margaret Waller married Sir William Courtenay in 1648. The Patronage is still held by the Earls of Devon.'

Then follows a chronological record of the Abbots of Torre and Rectors of Wolborough which contains the name of one William Yeo, appointed in 1648 and ejected in 1662.

Church and Chapel

Beginnings of Nonconformity

William Yeo was ejected from the living of Wolborough for refusing to conform to the laws of the Church of England. An article in **TDA** in 1884 says that "When William Yeo came to Newton Abbot 'he found the town very ignorant and profane', but that through his labours 'the people became very intelligent, serious and pious'. He appears to have been a terror to evildoers for on Sundays, to prevent the profanation of the Sabbath, he would walk round the town accompanied by the constable after public worship.'" It is perhaps more likely that William Yeo was ejected from Wolborough because the authorities felt threatened by his refusal to accept a state-controlled church rather than because of his attempts to chasten the inhabitants of Newton Abbot.

He and his supporters used to meet, by night, in a pit in Bradley Woods which became known as Puritan's Pit. The article in **TDA** records that an order of sessions was made at Michaelmas 1683 offering a reward of 40s. to anyone who apprehended a dissenting minister. Following this, a constable persuaded William Yeo to hide in a snow-covered field to escape arrest. This was one incident of many in which he was forced to flee from his family. Nevertheless, he always managed to avoid imprisonment. At the Midsummer Sessions for Devon in 1689, it was certified that the house of William Yeo be used as a place of religious worship under the Toleration Act passed in that year. Soon afterwards a chapel was built in Wolborough Street and William Yeo ministered there as a Presbyterian until 1699 when he died at the age of 82, having served the town for 53 years.

Today a plaque may be seen in the porch of the lychgate at Wolborough Church which previously belonged to the former United Reformed Church in Queen Street. It reads as follows: To the honoured memory of the Revd. William Yeo, MA, sometime Rector of this Parish. On the passing of the Act of Uniformity in the year 1662, he with a noble conscience, resigned his living, and, to avoid the persecution so rife in those troublous times, met his sympathising parishioners by night in Bradley Woods, for the worship of God, until a Chapel was built in Wolborough Street at which he became the Minister and thus the founder of Nonconformity in this Town. Born at Totness 1617, died 1699. This Tablet is erected by his descendants of the fifth generation, 1875.'

Presbyterians, Congregationalists and Baptists

William Yeo's first Presbyterian chapel stood on the site of 51, Wolborough Street. A second chapel stood on the site of number 68 and the congregations of both later joined together at Pound Chapel. Pound Chapel and the schools connected with it were endowed by Hannah Maria Bearne in 1788 who also provided an annual income for its minister. Pound Chapel was so named because it faced the animal pound of the old Newton Abbot market in Wolborough Street (hence also Pound Place). Pound Chapel was demolished in 1835 and replaced the following year by Salem Chapel, since demolished. Its name lives on in Salem Place.

The former Salem Chapel (left) now demolished and Schoolroom (right) adjacent to the street known as Salem Place.

Providence Chapel was built by Congregationalists in 1786 in a court in East Street next to the present Locomotive Inn. This chapel existed until its congregation joined the newly built Salem Chapel in 1843. A tablet commemorating Hannah Bearne's gift once hung in Pound Chapel, then Salem Chapel, and can now be seen in the entrance lobby of the

Church and Chapel

United Reformed Church in Queen Street, the members of whose former congregation are the indirect descendants of the dissenting William Yeo and his followers.

In 1972 the majority of Presbyterian and Congregational churches in England joined to form the United Reformed Church: the former United Reformed Church, built in 1875, in Queen Street was previously the Congregational Church, its elegant spire forming a prominent landmark. This church ceased to be a place of worship and now comprises offices for a legal practice, its congregation having joined the Methodist Church on the corner of the Avenue. The Presbyterians and the Congregationalists, together with the Baptists, formed the 'Three Denominations of Protestant Dissenters' who would not accept the rule of the monarchy in the Protestant Church.

The Baptists came to England from Holland at the beginning of the seventeenth century. Their followers built the first Baptist Church in Newton Abbot in 1697 which, according to **Rhodes**, 'consisted of four mud walls and two or three small windows and only about six or eight sittings'. **Stirling** records that in 1697 one Elizabeth Solman by deed of feoffment granted this chapel with its burial ground to its minister and members. The Baptist Chapel fell into disuse and was used as a store for arms and ammunition during the Napoleonic Wars. In 1819 the old chapel was demolished and rebuilt, although it still bears the date 1697. The present Baptist Chapel was erected in 1862, with a new frontage and schoolrooms added in 1894. The 1888 map shows the new building belonging to the General Baptists and the older one to the Particular Baptists, the latter being an old separatist group influenced by Calvinism. Today the older building in which the Particular Baptists once practised is used by the Spiritualists.

Methodists

John Wesley founded Methodism in the eighteenth century as a breakaway group from the established church and he and his followers converted many in the West Country to the new faith. Following the arrival of the railway in 1846, Newton Abbot experienced a considerable growth in the size of its population and of opportunities for worship in chapels which represented various Methodist sects in addition to the more traditional nonconformist religions. Many Methodist sects seceded during the first half of the nineteenth century, several of which reunited in the second half of that century and during the last century. The Wesleyans' first chapel was built in 1813 on the north side of Mill Lane near the Palk and Pinsent Brewery. They later moved to a new place of worship which was built in Courtenay Street in 1848 and which later became the Town Hall. This chapel was in turn superseded by a large new church on the opposite side of Courtenay Street, its former site at present occupied by Woolworths. A small Wesleyan Chapel was built in Keyberry Road, Decoy, in 1909.

The United Free Church was built in 1854 and occupied the building in Courtenay Street now used by Ex Sports. The large inscription 'Invertere Buildings' set in the limestone and brick façade indicates an intermediate use of this building by the firm of coat manufacturers who established themselves in the town in 1904. They later moved to Yorkshire but returned to the town, to Brunel Road, after World War II, finally moving to Scotland in the 1980s.

The Bible Christian Jubilee Chapel was built in 1865 with an adjoining Minister's residence on the corner of The Avenue and stood on the site of the present Methodist Church.

Other Denominations

There were several other nonconformist chapels. The Gospel Hall stood next to Bearne's School in Queen Street and its pitched roof can be seen today jutting above one side of the low, horizontal block of the Argos store. A former Unitarian Chapel, later occupied by the Jehovah's Witnesses and acquired by the Co-operative Society in 1984 for use as a Chapel of Rest, stands in Albany Street.

The Starkite Chapel was built in 1857, with the Philadelphia Hall, in Queen Street; this sect was so named because it was founded by someone called Stark. I have been unable to find any reference to this person. The Starkite Chapel was later used by the Unitarians.

The Plymouth Brethren were founded in that city in 1830 and a Brethren Chapel was built in Newton Abbot in 1859, by which time the

Church and Chapel

Brethren had split to form the Open Brethren and the Exclusive Brethren. Today the Christian Brethren meet at Prospect Chapel in East Street. The Assemblies of God, or Pentecostal Church, opened a new premises in Exeter Road in 1991.

Victorian revivalism made its mark on Newton Abbot in the shape of the Salvation Army which founded its citadel in Union Street. It is perhaps surprising that, in the once thriving industrial town of Newton Abbot, Quakers were apparently never sufficiently thick on the ground to establish a Meeting House.

The Roman Catholics made a belated post-Reformation comeback with the building of St. Joseph's Church in Queen Street in 1870. Prior to this, Catholics had to travel to the Catholic sanctuary at Ugbrooke House.

The Established Church

The Church of England had not been completely somnolent during this frenzy of nonconformist expansion. The Earl of Devon financed the building of St. Paul's Church in Devon Square in 1862. This church has a cruciform shape and is in the Early English style. It is attractively situated in a green square surrounded by some of Newton Abbot's finest town houses of the same period. All Saints Mission Chapel, otherwise known at the time as the Railway Mission, stands in Osborne Street. It is now incorporated into All Saints Primary School but is still recognisable as a chapel, particularly as it is approached from Chapel Road. St. Mary's in Abbotsbury was opened in 1906, as I have already mentioned, and an Anglican Mission, St. Michael and All Angels, was built in Kingskerswell Road, Decoy, and opened in 1910.

Since 1918

The last century witnessed the growth of the residential area of Buckland and Milber and the inclusion of the Parish of Milber within the boundaries of the Newton Abbot Urban District Council. A Mission Room was opened in Milber in 1930 to cater for the needs of a growing population. From this date Rev W. Keble Martin held services there. In

1931 Keble Martin, immortalised by his beautiful colour illustrations of British flora, experienced a particularly vivid dream in which he saw himself conducting a service in a new church of quite radical design. Keble Martin remembered the details and presented his idea to his architect brother who thought them feasible.

St. Luke's Milber, Keble Martin's 'Dream Church'

The main feature of this church is a central nave from which radiate at oblique angles a north and south nave and a Lady Chapel and Vestry. The altar is close to all parts of the church and all members of the congregation have an unimpeded view of the altar. This is how St. Luke's in Milber, the 'Dream Church', was conceived. Construction work soon began on the new church although the building was not completed until well after the Second World War.

The Bible Christians and Wesleyan Methodists united in 1932 to form the Methodist Church in Great Britain as it now exists. The two respective churches were replaced in the late 1960s by the Methodist Church on the corner of the Avenue, where the old grey limestone Bible Christian Jubilee Chapel had once stood. Soon after, a Methodist Chapel opened in Buckland.

Two further religious groups in Newton Abbot are the Jehovah's Witnesses who meet in their Kingdom Hall beside the former United Reformed Church (once Congregational) in Queen Street, and the Church of Jesus Christ and Latter Day Saints (Mormons) which has its fine, albeit stereotyped new Temple in Milber overlooking Pennin roundabout.

10

Some of the Town's Institutions

Schools

Newton Abbot's primary schools today include Bearne's, Wolborough, All Saints, St. Joseph's and Highweek in the town and Decoy, Milber and Bradley Barton in outlying areas. Bearne's School was founded by Maria Hannah Bearne who, in 1788, left a trust fund to maintain a charity school. The original school was situated in Wolborough Street next to the Salem Chapel. The present school building in Queen Street was erected in 1858 and enlarged in 1884. By Miss Bearne's bequest, pupils were not restricted to any particular Protestant sect but were to be accepted on condition that their parents attended some place of worship on Sundays. In the early days each child was presented with a Bible and remained at the school for four years.

Wolborough Church of England School in Union Street was built in 1870 and enlarged in 1893 although its origins are to be found in Bell's School which was established in 1816. **Stirling** says of this school that 'It depends entirely for support on the gratuitous subscriptions and donations of the benevolent' and points out that although money was donated locally, the cost of building the school was 'aided by a grant of £100 from the parent society in London'. All Saints (Marsh) School in Osborne Street was built in 1875 and is connected to St. Paul's Church in Devon Square.

St. Joseph's Roman Catholic School in Coombeshead Road replaced the original school which adjoined the Catholic Church in Queen Street. Highweek School was endowed by a Highweek parishioner, Miss Eliza Fagan, in 1863 in order to provide pupils with a strict Church of England education. The school was built adjoining St. Mary's Chapel in Highweek Street and was opened in 1879 with various extensions built in the Edwardian era. A new Highweek Junior School for Girls was built in Coronation Road and one for boys just off Highweek Road, whilst the original buildings in Highweek Street were maintained for infants. Eventually all sections of the school combined at the enlarged site in Coronation Road, whilst the former Highweek Boys' School became Coombeshead Lower School. Bradley Barton Primary was opened in 1980 to serve the children of the then fast-growing area which surrounds it.

When the railway was built to provide an efficient means of communication with London and major towns in the south-west, Newton Abbot began to attract many wealthy and middle class families. During the building boom which followed, many detached villas to house such families were built on the hills surrounding the town. These families demanded a superior education for their children and many private schools were established towards the close of the nineteenth century to meet their needs. The oldest and most famous was without doubt Newton College, after which College Road on Wolborough Hill is named. Newton College was established in 1861 in a house in Courtenay Park, and it moved to its site in College Road in 1864. Building continued throughout the 1870s and 1880s and the 20 acres of grounds included a chapel, library, gymnasium, swimming pool, tennis courts, cricket pavilion and sanatorium.

Other private schools for boys included Wolborough Hill School, which was described in advertisements as 'A Preparatory School for the Public Schools and Navy', Newton Grammar School which was founded mainly on the initiative of Rev Tudor, then Rector of Wolborough, and was situated in a large house in Courtenay Park, and Bradley High School which gave 'Special Attention to Commercial Subjects'. Private schools for girls included Fortescue House Girls' School in Forde Park, St. Bernard's School for Girls on Wolborough Hill, Fordeleigh College for Girls at numbers 2 and 3 Clifton Villas, Torquay Road, Newton Abbot High School in Courtenay Park and Hillside School 'for the Daughters of Gentlemen' on Wolborough Hill.

The Science, Art and Technical Schools adjoining the Passmore Edwards Public Library in Bank Street were financed by Devon County Council, were opened in 1904 and are described in the next chapter. The

Some of the Town's Institutions

Secondary School in Exeter Road was opened in 1915 and later became Newton Abbot Grammar School when Highweek Secondary Modern Schools were opened. Secondary education in Newton Abbot was reorganised on comprehensive lines during the mid-1970s. The Grammar School became Knowles Hill Comprehensive and, with Coombeshead Comprehensive, shares the facilities for art and sport at Dyrons Schools complex built in the grounds of Dyrons House, the latter forming a sixth-form college for Knowles Hill.

Seale Hayne Agricultural College stands back from the Ashburton Road about three miles out of Newton Abbot. The College was founded under the will of the Rt Hon Charles Seale Hayne (1833-1903) who was a local landowner and Member of Parliament for the Ashburton Division. The main buildings, arranged in the form of a quadrangle, were completed in 1919, its first agricultural students being admitted the following year, and quickly earned a high reputation. During World War II it was taken over by the Women's Land Army. Latterly it has been subsumed into the University of Plymouth which, amidst considerable controversy, closed it in 2005. At the time of writing it is employed as a centre for police training.

Almshouses

Almshouses were generally founded to provide shelter for needy persons by the charity of their more wealthy fellows. Prior to their dissolution, many homeless families and individuals found refuge in the monasteries which were scattered across the country.

There are several sets of almshouses in Newton Abbot but those with the longest history are Gilbert's (or Gilberd's) Almshouses in Exeter Road. They were endowed in 1538 by John Gilbert, the great-uncle of Sir Humphrey Gilbert of Compton Castle, to provide a refuge for lepers. The original establishment consisted of four houses and a chapel, the chapel later being converted into a fifth house. All the houses are reputed to have had sloping floors in order that they could be more easily washed out, presumably to protect Newtonians from the 'unclean' occupants of the lazar houses.

The name of Wain Lane, which once connected Gilbert's Almshouses with Highweek Road, has an interesting derivation. I have found reference to the theory that Wain Lane owes its name to the fact that a haywain maker once had his workshop situated here. I have also been informed that the 'Wain' of Wain Lane is derived from the word 'wen' which the dictionary gives as meaning a 'more or less permanent tumour of benign character on scalp or other part of body', and hence its possible connection with the lazar houses. It is interesting to discover that Wain Lane is given as 'Wen Lane' on the Town Survey of 1843. Gilbert's Almshouses were rebuilt in the nineteenth century and again in 1979.

In 1576 Robert Hayman endowed properties in East Street 'for the better maintenance and relief of poor people'. These properties included almshouses which were rebuilt in 1845 and survive today as the terrace of four cottages in grey limestone opposite Newton Abbot Hospital in East Street. In Torquay Road, on the corner of Church Road, stand four almshouses known as the Lady Lucy Reynell Clergy Widows' houses. These were endowed by Lady Lucy Reynell, wife of Sir Richard Reynell of Forde House. The original houses were built in 1640 but rebuilt in 1790 and refurbished in 1846. Lady Lucy intended them to accommodate four widows, 'the relicts of preaching ministers, left poor, without a house of their own'. The houses bore the following inscription:

THE WIDOWE'S HOUSE, 1638
Is't strange a prophets widow poore sovld be?
Yf strange, then is the scripture strange to thee.

This no doubt ensured that no rich preaching ministers' widows would squeeze through the portals of Reynell's Almshouses. A tablet in the vestry at Wolborough Church describes additional qualifications that the poor widows should fulfil:

'That the said wyddows there placed shall be such as shal 3 days in every week frequent Church and divine service, and shal be noe gadders, gosappers, tatlers, tale bearers, nor given to reproachful words, nor abusers of anye. That none of them keep above one servant maide to attend them, and that noe man be lodged in any of the said houses'

Some of the Town's Institutions

Mackrell's Almshouses in Totnes Road are undoubtedly the most noticeable of all Newton Abbot's almshouses. They are to be seen on the north side of the Totnes Road just before Baker's Park. A long terrace with its porches and chimneys and gables solidly built in grey Devonian limestone stands out impressively against the green hill which rises steeply behind.

These almshouses were endowed by Thomas Mackrell who was born in Newton Abbot and, as a child, played near this very spot. He made his fortune as a chemist in Barnstaple and decided to purchase the land he remembered from his childhood to provide a site on which to erect some almshouses. The original terrace was built in 1874 and over the entrance in the middle of the block is the following inscription:

> By the Grace of God
> The Mackrell Almshouses
> Erected and Endowed
> In the year of our Lord 1874

Thomas later died and left his fortune to his sister Miss Sophia. When she in turn died in 1894 the money reverted to the trustees for the purpose of erecting more almshouses. A further block was built in exactly the same style and adjoins the existing terrace. A second entrance and inscription records this extension to Mackrell's Almshouses.

The Workhouse

Each parish supported its own poor until the Poor Law Amendment Act of 1834. Newton Abbot, or Wolborough Parish, maintained a poorhouse which was situated on the north side of East Street between the Dartmouth Inn and the Devon Arms. The cellar of the Devon Arms was used as the oakum picking room, where paupers were set the painful task of unwinding the tangled fibres of old ropes to provide material to caulk the seams of wooden ships. **Rhodes** describes the poorhouse accounts ledger from 1781 to 1800 at some length.

If Wolborough poorhouse had a famous inmate, she must be Kitty Jay, the basis of the Dartmoor legend of Jay's Grave wherein suicide victim

129

A Book of Newton Abbot

Kitty is said to be interred at a parish crossroads. An imaginative and well written account of Kitty's life and death, based on historical facts as far as they are known, is to be found in the book *An Angel from Your* Door by Hardy scholar, the late Lois Deacon. According to her book, Kitty was born in 1790 and was rescued as a foundling in Keyberry Street (later East Street). She was taken in by the Wolborough Workhouse and later indentured by a Dartmoor farmer. Here she fell in love with a young man on a neighbouring farm, became pregnant and eventually hung herself.

Shortly before I left Newton Abbot I received a letter at the library from one Joe Keeton in Liverpool who was studying the phenomenon of regressive hypnosis. One of his subjects, a nurse from the Wirral, had regressed and adopted the personality of Kitty Jay. This young woman had no previous knowledge of Kitty Jay and, indeed, had never even visited Devon. Keeton's enquiry led to a television programme in Plymouth to which I was invited, along with other interested parties including the writer Colin Wilson. Joe Keeton hypnotised his subject who gradually assumed the character of Kitty Jay, adopting a Devon accent and even using dialect words in use around 1800. He led her through the events leading up to the fatal moment, when she grasped the perceived noose around her neck in a last attempt to reverse her action. At this moment Keeton brought the young woman back to consciousness. Keeton himself had no explanation for this phenomenon, just the ability to 'take people back to past lives'. It was all very spooky: inexplicable, but convincing nevertheless. Keeton later co-authored a book, *Encounters with the Past: How man can relive and experience history* (Sidgwick and Jackson, 1979) which contains case studies of certain of his subjects, though not the young woman who had become Kitty Jay.

Newton Bushel, or Highweek Parish, had its own poorhouse in Exeter Road, close to the former junction of Exeter and Highweek Roads. The 1834 Act decreed that several parishes should form a union to be administered by a board of governors which would be assisted by paid relieving officers. The Newton Abbot Union was constituted in 1836 when a meeting was held at the Globe Inn which was attended by representatives from 39 parishes. It was decided to build a new workhouse in East Street, Newton Abbot, to accommodate local paupers and those from Torquay, Teignmouth, Ashburton and the many villages in the rural district.

According to **Rhodes**, the new workhouse was intended as a 'means of

Some of the Town's Institutions

dealing with the mass of able bodied pauperism, which was threatening to become a danger to the community'. Such people found increased opportunities for regular employment in the latter half of the nineteenth century and the workhouse became 'more and more a hospital for the sick and infirm, and a place for the large number of aged poor who have no friends or relatives to take charge of them'.

The Workhouse, East Street

The erection of the new workhouse went ahead and the first paupers moved in during the year 1839. In White's 1850 *Directory of Devon*, Newton Abbot Workhouse is described as follows:

> 'pleasantly situated on the eastern side of the town, and is one of the best in England, both in external appearance and internal arrangement. The various woods, yards etc. occupy nearly 2 acres and attached to it are about 2 acres of garden ground.'

Here able-bodied paupers could grow vegetables and keep animals while their children were given lessons: the boys learned gardening and shoe making and the girls housewifery.

'ONLY SOME UNION BABIES!

Only some 'Union Babies!' well,
    I know that cynics say:
They 're only little 'pauper kids',
    The children of the gay!
But say 'tis true: what matters it?
    What diff'rence can it make?
No child should be neglected, tho'
    Its parents it forsake!

All children claim, and 'tis their right,
    'A chance' to get them through the fight
Of life! and these poor little chicks,
    Tho' born within some Workhouse bricks,
Should have such chances we can give,
    As those who in more comfort live.

Whether child of the poor or child of the rich,
    Whether born in a palace, or born in a ditch;
Give each one 'a chance' regardless of rank,
    Humanity cries 'tis her we must thank;
Give each a fair start that whatever the pace,
    Each poor little kid has a chance in the race!

Some of the Town's Institutions

In 1842 the inmates numbered 285; at the turn of the century there were between 350 and 400. During this period of growth in numbers, facilities became inadequate and the house understaffed. In 1893 some new members were elected to the Board of Guardians. Among these was one Dr. J W Ley, a local general practitioner, who inaugurated an enquiry into some alarming accounts of cruel treatment to many of the inmates, particularly the sick, imbeciles and children. As a result, the Matron and other officials were forced to resign, the staff was increased and many of the children were boarded out with foster parents while others were housed in cottage homes, for which purpose four houses were acquired.

During the Great War one ward of the workhouse was taken over by the Army and used as a Military Hospital. After the war many paupers returned but were driven out once more during the Second World War when the workhouse was converted into a Hospital for the Royal Navy. Some returned in 1945 but their numbers gradually declined until the old workhouse building was converted into the geriatric section of Newton Abbot Hospital, which it remains today.

Dr J W Ley (pictured opposite) published a couple of books during his lifetime. One was a collection of verse, many poems of which are based upon his experiences whilst living and working in Newton Abbot, and the other a book of prose stories and reminiscences of his days as a medical student in London and as a General Practitioner in Devon. His poem, 'Only Some Union Babies', quoted here, expresses Dr Ley's deep sense of concern for the plight of the pauper children of Newton Abbot Workhouse.

The Hospital

A Cottage Hospital was built in 1873 in East Street and was maintained by voluntary subscriptions and donations. It accommodated only thirteen patients which was soon found to be quite inadequate for the needs of Newton Abbot and District.

A new larger hospital was made possible by two generous donors. Mr D R Scratton, squire of the Ogwells, presented a site in East Street near the Baptist Chapel and adjoining the Union Workhouse. Mrs Emmeline Fisher of Abbotsbury House, who at the time had just been left a widow,

A Book of Newton Abbot

bore the cost of building the first stage of the new hospital as a memorial to her late husband. Mrs Scratton laid the foundation stone in 1896, Mrs Fisher herself having died in the meantime; she also declared the hospital open in 1898.

A fund was set up to celebrate the Diamond Jubilee of Queen Victoria and this raised the sum of £1,044. For fifty years until the National Health Service was established in 1948 and the State assumed ownership and control, Newton Abbot Hospital was run on an entirely voluntary basis. One of the great events in Newton Abbot's calendar was Hospital Saturday which was held annually in order to raise funds for the hospital. A procession through the town was followed by collectors who sometimes raised £500. There was often a firework display in the evening and food and drink was served in the grounds of Dyrons House, which was the home of Mr Charles Lane Vicary, Chairman of the Hospital Saturday Committee.

Newton Abbot Hospital. East Street

Rhodes lists the names of Newtonians who donated large amounts to the hospital funds between 1873 and 1903, when his book on Newton Abbot was written. Among these are the firms of Vicarys and Watts, Blake and Bearne, Mr Scratton who bequeathed an orchard behind the hospital,

Some of the Town's Institutions

Thomas Mackrell and later the two Misses Mackrell, Rev Tudor, Rector of Wolborough, Mrs Fisher, Mr R H M Baker, at one time Clerk to the Local Board whom we must also thank for the gift of Baker's Park, and Dr H B Mapleton, a former Medical Officer of Health for Newton Abbot and District after whom Mapleton House in Ashburton Road is named. Many well healed local residents subscribed a fixed amount on a regular annual basis and there was a scheme whereby every man who earned less than £5 per week could insure hospital treatment for himself and his family by the payment of 2d per week. Funds raised by voluntary means paid for a Radiological Department, which in 1914 was the first one to be established in the South West Region. In 1927 hospital extensions were opened by HRH Edward, Prince of Wales who was annoyed at being kept waiting in the rain before being presented with the key.

Newton Abbot Hospital's original handsome façade, an attractive mixture of architectural styles, is now somewhat marred by the imposition of assorted extensions and outbuildings but the old Union Workhouse, now the Geriatric Unit, is still an impressive building seen from Western Road or East Street. Newton Abbot's Isolation Hospital on the Totnes Road was built in 1902 and extended in 1909. It is now known as Brunel Lodge.

A large new hospital is planned to replace these ageing facilities to be built at Jetty Marsh in 2007/8.

It is interesting that so many of Newton Abbot's public amenities have in the past been provided on a voluntary basis, either by the generosity of individuals or by public subscription. This holds true not only for its primary schools, almshouses and the hospital but also for Baker's Park, its public library and, more recently, its swimming pool at Pennin (now lost) and community centre.

11

Newton Abbot Public Library and Passmore Edwards

At the junction of Bank Street and Market Street stands a building which must surely be one of the most impressive in Newton Abbot. This building is really two buildings, as we may discern by reading the lettering which circumscribes their shared frontage between the ground and first floors. The double-fronted building facing Bank Street is the 'Passmore Edwards Public Library' and the building on the corner is the 'Science, Art and Technical Schools'. Inscribed on a granite plinth on the left side of the double oak doors of the library are the following words:

> THIS STONE WAS LAID
> BY THE DONOR
> J. PASSMORE EDWARDS ESQ.
> 9th OCTOBER 1902
> CHARLES GEORGE VICARY ESQ.
> CHAIRMAN OF THE PUBLIC
> LIBRARY COMMITTEE

Above the door and set in an ornate, terracotta moulding are these words:

Newton Abbot Public Library and Passmore Edwards

> THIS BUILDING WAS PRESENTED
> TO THE TOWN BY
> J. PASSMORE EDWARDS
> IN MEMORY OF HIS MOTHER

The Science, Art and Technical Schools which has its entrance at the corner, displays a similar granite plinth at the left hand of its entrance and bears the following inscription:

> THE RIGHT HONBLE ALBERT EDMUND 3rd EARL OF MORLEY
> CHAIRMAN OF THE DEVON COUNTY COUNCIL
> 9th OCTOBER 1902
> WILLIAM VICARY ESQ., J.P., C.C.
> CHAIRMAN OF THE NEWTON ABBOT URBAN DISTRICT
> COUNCIL

Thus we can see that these two foundation stones were laid on the same day and that both representatives of the local council were members of Newton's mill owning family, the Vicarys. I do not pro pose to delve into the life of the then 3rd Earl of Morley but to take space, instead, to portray a little of the life of an outstanding Victorian philanthropist, J. Passmore Edwards.

John Passmore Edwards was born in Blackwater, a small village between Redruth and Truro, in Cornwall, in 1823. His mother was a native of Newton Abbot and lived in East Street. The town survey of 1843 shows a small property, where East Street curves round towards Bank Street, somewhere in the midst of Austin's, marked 'Passmore'. Edwards adopted his mother's maiden name as his own middle name.

His father was a carpenter by trade, and a Cornishman. John, his three brothers and his father and mother, lived in a small four-roomed cottage in Blackwater, but soon his father built a larger house nearby for which he obtained a public house licence. Father brewed his own beer which he sold on the premises and supplied to some of the beershops in the adjacent village. Later still, John's father gave up brewing and public house keeping and became a market gardener.

Passmore Edwards wrote a very brief autobiography in 1905 at the age

A Book of Newton Abbot

of 82, entitled *A Few Footprints*. In this he recalls that 'books in my father's house were few, and fewer still in most of the houses in the village; and the books within reach were more theological than interesting.' Young Edwards grew up to become a journalist and founder of a publishing empire, in which roles he promoted the interests of world peace and social reform. In his book he declares that 'in all my experience as editor of or contributor to newspapers or magazines, I never wrote a sentence or passed a sentence on to the printers, that I did not think true, and useful because true.' One wonders how many of today's newspapermen and women could say the same.

In 1868, Passmore Edwards received and accepted an invitation to contest Truro in a General Election. He stood as an Independent against both Conservative and Liberal Candidates and his manifesto pledged support for universal education for children, universal suffrage and equal representation of constituencies in Parliament, a policy of non-intervention in wars and one of arbitration rather than conflict in the settlement of national disputes, abolition of blood sports, an end to university entrance on religious grounds, abolition of capital punishment, better housing for the working classes and financial protection for trade unions. We can see from this list how radical and progressive Passmore Edwards was in his views.

Mr Edwards did not win Truro although he did fight and win Salisbury in 1880. Having gained a seat in Parliament, he became pretty sceptical about the whole business of professional politics. The following passage from his book reveals his views on this matter:

> 'I did not find Parliament such a fruitful field for usefulness as I expected.... It appeared to me that as soon as a majority of members got into Parliament, after a General Election, they lost much of the zeal they displayed for public interests on the hustings.... It mattered little what was said in debate on either side, in nine cases out of ten members voted on party lines in obedience to party discipline. As a rule an ordinary member of Parliament is only a cog of a wheel of a party machine.... As a rule rich and titled men can no more represent working men than able working men can fitly represent the rich and titled.... There ought to have been two hundred such men working men), and then we should have a more real

Newton Abbot Public Library and Passmore Edwards

representation, and the nation, I believe, would soon become stronger and happier.'

What Passmore Edwards remains most well known for, of course, is his philanthropy and the various institutions which he paid for in London and south-west England, and which today stand as monuments to one man's deeply held conviction to help his fellow man. His thoughts on this activity are eloquently expressed in this passage from his book:

> 'Having gathered, I determined to put into action what I had long nurtured in thought and use certain means at my disposal for the general good. The chief question was: How could this be best done to produce the best result?... As I had accumulated mainly by the labours of others, I thought, and think, it was only reasonable and just that others should share in the garnered result; and to act accordingly was a duty and a privilege – a duty as a citizen and a privilege as a man. I also thought, and think, that the great working class – the foundation and bulwark of national existence and the chief producer of national necessities – are entitled to primary consideration in such matters. I consequently decided to do what I could for their welfare, and thought the best' thing to do was to help them help each other; and that this could be most productively done by promoting institutional activity.'

Newton Abbot Public Library was the visible result of such thinking.

Andrew Carnegie, making a speech whilst opening a Passmore Edwards Library at Plaistow, said of Passmore Edwards:

> 'Mr Passmore Edwards was a man who spent little upon himself, and was the liver of a quiet, unostentatious and inexpensive life, disdaining luxury and religiously devoting his entire surplus for the good of man.... Mr Edwards was a leading and true disciple of the gospel of wealth, which holds the duty of the rich to live simply, to scorn delights, and live laborious days, in the service of their fellow-men.'

A Book of Newton Abbot

In all, Passmore Edwards financed the building of 72 useful institutions, of which 23 were Free Libraries. The remainder included village institutions (his first gift was such to his home village of Blackwater), hospitals, convalescent homes, children's homes, technical schools and homes for epileptics.

Passmore Edwards was twice offered a knighthood, which he declined on both occasions. This provides sufficient evidence to counter the widespread notion that Victorian philanthropists were patronising eccentrics, whose real motivation was public recognition and self aggrandisement. Such an image could not be further from the truth in the case of Passmore Edwards.

He died in 1911 at the age of 88.

M r Parker, a member of Newton Abbot Council, met Passmore Edwards when he was seated next to him at a Masonic dinner in London in 1901. When Mr Edwards discovered that Mr Parker was a Newtonian, he immediately told him of his intention to build some useful institution in the town in memory of his mother. His first idea was to build a hospital but when he learned that Newton Abbot already possessed an adequate hospital he offered to present the town with a Free Library providing a site was found. There were two small libraries in Newton at the time. One was established in 1836 by the Society for the Attainment of Useful Knowledge, the other was the GWR Mechanics Institute library which was opened in 1877, in the then defunct atmospheric pumping station tower. Both libraries together only opened for three hours weekly on two evenings.

On receipt of the news of Edwards' generous offer the Council proposed that a Technical School be built with the library. The site chosen at the junction of Highweek Street and Market Street was known as Harvey's Corner and had been purchased by the Council for road improvements. The cost of building the Free Library was £2,290.

Passmore Edwards donated £2,500 which presumably included the cost of fixtures and fittings and perhaps some books. £1,200 was raised by public subscription, including a gift of £200 from the Rt. Hon. Seale Hayne, MP which, together with £2,700 from the County Council, paid for the Technical School. Passmore Edwards travelled down from London to attend the foundation stone laying ceremony on October 9th, 1902.

Newton Abbot Public Library and Passmore Edwards

This was followed by luncheon in the Alexandra Hall for the guest of honour and all the nobility and gentry in the district while the Volunteer Band played in the market place. According to a report in the *Mid Devon and Newton Times*, in his speech Passmore Edwards spoke of his mother and was so overcome with emotion that he could not continue.

The library and technical schools building was designed by the distinguished Victorian architect and Cornishman, Sylvanus Trevail. Construction commenced in 1902 and was completed in 1904. In 1903 Mr Trevail shot himself dead in a railway train in a tunnel near Bodmin Road Station. His work on the Newton Abbot library and schools building was completed by his only assistant, Alfred Cornelius of Teignmouth, who took over Trevail's practice in Truro.

The buildings were completed in accordance with Trevail's plans with the exception that the clock turret was omitted, which was to have surmounted the corner. The style is Renaissance and is of an elaborate nature. The front elevation is of worked grey limestone with terracotta mouldings used in the windows, fascias, doorways and general ornamentation. Over the central windows of the Schools there is a pediment with the carved arms of Newton Abbot and Newton Bushel; these are also represented in mosaic in the floor of the entrance hall of the Schools. The spandrell of the arch is decorated with figures representing art and learning.

The upper floors of the Newton Abbot Science, Art and Technical Schools next to the library now house the Adult and Community Learning Centre. The original entrance to the library in Highweek Street is no longer used and the Schools entrance on the corner now provides access to both buildings. A description of the original function of this building helps us to conceive the original Schools. The ground floor had a room for technical drawing and building construction, a room for science and technical classes and a dark room for photography. Cases on the walls of the staircase and first landing contained a collection of fossils and corals presented by William Vicary, led to rooms on the first floor housing a chemical laboratory, a physical laboratory and a science lecture and demonstrating room with semi-circular seating, raised in tiers. The top floor was reserved for art classes – for drawing, painting, clay modelling and wood carving activities.

The library was opened in 1904 by the Rt. Hon. Redvers Buller, who

A Book of Newton Abbot

gained fame in the South African War. A report in the local paper at the time states the following:

> 'The building represents a distinct advance on libraries presented by Mr Passmore Edwards to other towns. Everything is of the most up-to-date character, and it is understood that the system for the lending library will be the very latest type, and as such will afford borrowers and librarian the minimum of trouble.'

Nevertheless, the library that borrowers see today is utterly different in its internal organisation to the library that greeted Newtonians in 1904.

In those days you would enter the library to find a large general reading room through the swing doors on your right side, and a smaller magazine room on your left. Up three stairs you would find a door leading to the Ladies Reading Room. Further up the stairs, on reaching the first floor, you would find the librarian behind a counter and the book indicator boards. A glance at these boards would tell you which books were available. When you had made your choice you would fill in a form and hand it to the librarian who would dive into the book store to retrieve the requested volume. The book store is now the Reference Library.

This room was adjacent to the librarian's office, which is now houses the local collection. The present librarian's office was originally a committee room, no doubt used by various bodies of the Newton Abbot Urban District Council over the years, including the Library Committee. The top floor contained a flat used by a caretaker who looked after both the library and the schools next door.

Climbing the stairs to the first floor of the library you cannot fail to be impressed by the large windows rising from the half-landing. The coloured glass inserts revere Homer, Milton, Shakespeare and Literature and on the window-sill resides and sculpted bust of Passmore Edwards, looking like a cross between Karl Marx and Father Christmas, presented by Hexter, Humpherson & Co., Proprietors of the Royal Watcombe Quarry.

Cornishman William Maddern was Newton Abbot's first librarian. In those days it was the task of the librarian to appeal to all and sundry for books for his library. Concerts and plays were performed at the Alexandra Theatre to raise money for the library's book fund. Mr Maddern succeeded in securing many gifts of books, particularly from the Vicary family. The

Newton Abbot Public Library and Passmore Edwards

trustees of the British Museum donated 163 volumes and the Mechanics' Institute of the Great Western Railway gave a thousand books, the entire contents of its library. In the first year of operation, a ld. library rate produced £200. Fines brought in a further £24. This sum financed the year's activities, including the librarian's salary!

I received in 1980 an appreciative letter from William Maddern's son, W Graham Maddern, in which he recollects that Newton Abbot Council was sensitive to the librarian's lack of financial reward and gave him other odd jobs, such as Clerk to the Cemetery Committee, which served to boost his salary. He also recalls that his mother had to deputise for him when her husband was posted overseas in the First World War. Graham Maddern relished his weekend's delving into the *Illustrated London News, Tatler, Strand Magazine* and *Punch* amongst other periodicals which were brought home last thing on Saturday night (after 9.00pm) and returned first thing Monday morning.

My predecessor, Lilian Ridler, worked at Newton Abbot Library for a remarkable forty-three years. She joined the service in 1933 at the age of sixteen and retired in 1976, the year I replaced her. She wrote an interesting piece about her library experiences in the June 1976 issue of the *Devon Library Services Staff Magazine*, from which these extracts are quoted:

> The Lending Library was just one room, the area where fiction is now kept. In those unenlightened days only a small corner of the room was devoted to children. There was a reference room upstairs and the room which is now the Children's Library [today's Reference Library] was called the Little Theatre. In this room lectures were given to bored children who spent their time picking winkles out of shells with a pin. As a junior assistant I was supposed to keep them quiet whilst they were forced to listen to piano recitals and learned lectures. I also found it boring and had every sympathy with them.
>
> The room was also used as a theatre by the local amateur dramatic society. The changing rooms for the theatre now house the local history collection. This room was also used for the preparation of refreshments for any library meetings held at Newton Abbot, Many times I was aroused from my reveries by the sound and smell of milk boiling over. The

Librarian's office was a sacred precinct and we were only allowed in there if we were feeling unwell. At such times we were given Bovril and very stale wholemeal bread. This was a great cure for all our ills as we hated it. It was considered a great crime to stay at home.

This was a very leisurely time for we issued very few books but the hours were long and as I couldn't go home for lunch it seemed a long day for 12s.6d. per week.

The Librarian became ill and Lilian Ridler was put in charge in her absence. Encouraged by the Chairman of the town's Library Committee, the new librarian in charge proceeded to make changes:

First of all we roped off half the room used as a reading room [today's Reference Library] and converted it into a Children's department... By decorating the walls with cut-outs and illustrations it looked quite attractive. The children began to pour in which made things a little difficult as there were only two members of staff...

We became very daring and explored the Librarian's office where we found stacks of new books waiting to be dealt with from years back. We also discovered that there was quite a sum of money in the Book Fund that hadn't been spent. So we embarked on a spending spree. This brought in more borrowers. With the outbreak of war in 1939 we were swamped with evacuees and no money to spend.

Lilian Ridler was appointed Librarian in 1947 and:

From then on it was one long battle to obtain money to fulfil even the most modest improvements. We battled on and I believe we didn't do too badly in the end for our issues increased from around 300 per day when I first started to over 1000 on a weekday and well over 2000 on Saturdays. We also managed to obtain a room for a Children's Library and start a local collection and gradually the staff increased from three to seven.

Newton Abbot Public Library and Passmore Edwards

With the demise of Newton Abbot Urban District Council in 1974, Newton Abbot ceased to be an independent library authority and the town's library fell under the control of Devon County Library Services, a source of considerable controversy at the time. Until 1980, Newton Abbot acted as the central library for Newton Abbot Division, with responsibility for nine smaller branch libraries in communities as far away as Chagford and Buckfastleigh. The library service was reorganised once more in 1980, when Newton Abbot lost its divisional status, a development which contributed to my departure. 1998 witnessed the creation of the Torbay and Plymouth Unitary Authorities so that Devon Library Services lost responsibility for those two urban areas. What remained was carved up into eight Districts. At the time of writing a question mark hangs over the survival of up to twelve branch libraries in the country, including some in the former Newton Abbot Division, and the organisation of what remains is once again in the melting pot.

Since my departure as Newton Abbot Librarian in 1980 the service has improved dramatically. The entrance to the Library has shifted from Highweek Street to an entrance shared with Adult Education on the corner of Highweek Street and Sherborne Road. The internal spaces have been reallocated so that the Lending Library, including Children's, is on the ground floor (and how marvellous that the Library is now carpeted throughout!) On the first floor, what in my day was the Children's Library is now an enlarged Reference Library, equipped with a suite of computers. The former Reference Library now houses the Railway Studies Library which opened in 1993. A Town Museum was housed on the top floor for a brief time in the 1980s before it moved to its present, much more generous accommodation adjacent to the Town Council offices at 2 St Paul's Road (the former home of the YMCA). This includes the Great Western Railway Museum.

Newton Abbot Library has successfully reinvented itself over the century since it opened. It is heartening that Passmore Edwards' generous gift to the town remains welcoming and well used.

12

Town Trails

Walking around Newton Abbot was my starting point in finding the information for writing this book. I originally devised these town trails in order to take children from the library to see parts of the town which, perhaps, they had not seen before. Each trail is between one and two miles in length and returns to the starting point at St. Leonard's Tower. We found that about one and half hours are needed to complete each one. This allows time to appreciate all there is to see and time to rest at a suitable point about half way along each trail. It is not an easy task to devise circular trails on a set theme but the contents given here approximate to their titles, 'Highweek', 'Wolborough' and 'Industrial Newton'.

1   HIGHWEEK

St. Leonard's Tower

Prince William made his famous proclamation here in 1688 and this fact is recorded on a commemorative stone at the base of the Tower.

Bank Street

Turning into Bank Street you pass the old Post Office (now the Mitre Bookshop) on your right and can soon see the ornate and colourful façade of the Adult Education Centre, formerly the Science, Art and Technical Schools, and the Passmore Edwards Public Library. Opposite the library, note the attractive brick house, known as Lovegate House, with handsome granite portico.

Highweek Street

Just past the library you can see Minerva House with its curved bay windows; the statue of Minerva, which formerly surmounted the building, has been removed. This street was an important thoroughfare in the days when Highweek Street allowed the only access to the Exeter Road.

Continue up here past the Swan Inn and the entrance to the Cattle Market, past old St Mary's Church, now happily converted into living accommodation after many years of neglect, to reach the crossroads, with the new Highweek Way on the left (leading to the older Bradley Lane) and Halcyon Road on the right.

Town Trails

Footpath
On the right past the entrance to the old Exeter Road, which is now a cul-de-sac, like Highweek Road opposite, is a footpath which begins at a pair of large, stone gateposts. This was the drive to former Abbotsbury House on Treacle Hill, a site now occupied by the church of St. Mary's of Abbotsbury.

Waverley Road
Turn left where the footpath emerges into Waverley Road, then left into Abbotsbury Road.

Exeter Road
Here you take the subway under the main road opposite Knowles Hill School and walk towards the roundabout. Note Gilberd's Almshouses on the opposite side; these were rebuilt in 1979. Dyrons House is on the left. Dyrons Centre was opened in 1975 as a facility for the two secondary schools. A swimming pool was added in 1989 to replace the abandoned open air pool built in 1935, at Penn Inn. Cross the road and carry on up Exeter Road by the pavement on the left.

Exeter Road
You approach the junction with Jetty Marsh Road Road, not so long ago a little used lane which has since been widened to divert traffic coming to and from Kingsteignton and points west of the town centre. Sandford Orleigh House, the former home of Sir Samuel Baker and now converted into flats, is to the right. Carry on until you reach a track on the left. Turn in here and make for the hedged footpath which climbs steadily towards Highweek Church. The church occupies a peaceful hill-top site where you can take time to enjoy the views by walking round the churchyard.

Leave the lych gate on the far side and head towards the centre of Highweek village where you will find the Highweek Inn on your right. Beyond the Inn you bear left into Coombeshead Road.

Just past the entrance to Castlewood Avenue look out for a Public Footpath sign on your right. Follow this old way between private gardens – notice the fragments of slate underfoot indicating that the rock beneath is Devonian Slate. You descend to reach Ashburton Road –

Highweek Church, as seen emerging from the old coffin path

A Book of Newton Abbot

cross over (take care!) Continue in the same direction by the path on the far side until you reach Barton Drive. Turn left here and carry on until you spot the start of a footpath on the far side. Cross over to follow the beaten path as is rises through woods and then drops down beside Bradley Manor on your right.

Bradley Manor

Climb down some steps and over a stile towards the bridge on the mill leat. Here you can see a spring issuing into the leat and, a little farther on, the path bridges the Lemon and continues towards the gate house on the Totnes Road. The bridge on the leat is an ideal place to take a rest before turning back towards town. Bradley Meadow, the open space to your right, lies encircled by trees.

Find your way back to town by following the footpath along the side of the leat. Here you can see a sluice gate by means of which it is possible to regulate the flow of water. There is a channel which runs under the path to connect the leat with the Lemon which here runs nearby but at a lower level. The leat flows underground just before the former Bradley Mill is reached.

Bradley Lane

You enter Bradley Lane between the old buildings of the former woollen mills. These were rebuilt in 1883: you can see a commemorative tablet set into the wall bearing the initials J V & S: John Vicary & Sons, and the date.

Continue the walk along Bradley Lane. At the terrace of cottages where the mill leat reappears you turn right until you reach the Lemon. From here you turn left along a riverside path, beyond Highweek Way.

Here you will reach a couple of bridges over the Lemon, including Union Bridge. You can see the Lemon channelled underground, beneath Bank Street, before you return to that road and turn right towards St. Leonard's Tower.

View down the Teign estuary from footpath beside Highweek Church
Opposite: Looking back to Wolborough Church from the footpath

2 WOLBOROUGH

Wolborough Street
From St. Leonard's Tower you walk up Wolborough Street. There is much evidence to be seen in the buildings to your left of this street's origins in pre-Victorian times.

Look out 'The Tudor House' a large, detached house signified on its porch as 'Manor House A.D. 1534' which once housed the civil court of the Manor of Wolborough but is today the offices of the *Mid-Devon Advertiser*.

Number 83 was the house of John Lethbridge - his grave may be found in Wolborough churchyard.

Note, too, at number 2 Totnes Road, the blue plaque dedicated to former resident Oliver Heaviside (1850-1925) a pioneering scientist who lived here for 11 years.

At the end of the distinctive terrace forming Mackrell's Almshouses you take the path on the left which leads to Wolborough Church and is known as Church Path.

Church Path
You climb the path beside fields steadily uphill. At the path's summit you reach Coach Road.

Coach Road
Wolborough Barton, still a working farm, is opposite and the church of St. Mary's of Wolborough to the left. The overgrown hillocks opposite are the remains of a former sandpit.

Wolborough Hill
After visiting the church you go through the gate to the left of the churchyard and follow the path which curves away across the wide field before you, following a more or less even contour. Note how red the soil is hereabouts - an indication that the rock beneath is an outlier of New Red Sandstone - the same rock which forms the red cliffs of Teignmouth and Dawlish.

This path will lead you to the corner of a field of allotments whose boundary is marked by a line of Scots pines. This is probably the best point at which to take in the wonderful view from Wolborough Hill. From here you can see almost all of Newton Abbot, Highweek, Bradley Manor and Woods and much farther towards Dartmoor in the west and the Teign Estuary in the east.

After pausing to enjoy the view and perhaps rest your legs, continue along

A Book of Newton Abbot

the path, again following more or less the same contour until, after following a stone wall for some distance, you emerge at the top of Powderham Road. Here you turn right and left into Courtenay Road.

Courtenay Road

Continue along here and pause once more to enjoy the view over the town and beyond before turning left down a signposted footpath which leads downhill. A wooden fence soon gives way to concrete steps between stone walls and streets of old terraced houses, mostly brick-built, in contrast to the grey limestone employed in the rather older buildings of the hospital and former workhouse which can be seen from here.

Western Road

Follow the footpath until you reach Western Road which comprises a long, steeply staggered terrace of houses facing the boundary wall of Newton Abbot Hospital. About half way down, surmounting the wall, is an inscribed tablet which commemorates an agreement in 1897 between the Urban District Council and the Guardians of the Newton Abbot Union for sharing spring water which issues from Bowden Hill on which the workhouse was built.

East Street

Turn left into East Street, another ancient thoroughfare of Newton Abbot. On the far side of the road you can see Hayman's Almshouses and the Rope Walk, as well as Ye Olde Cider Bar, one of a handful of pubs in Britain licensed to sell only cider and wine, albeit not an ancient hostelry.

School Road

Turn right into School Road, past Wolborough School and the old Wolborough Parish Room and Soup Kitchen – the latter indicated by a tablet set high in the wall. Turn left into Union Street and left into Courtenay Street which leads you back to St. Leonard's Tower.

Kissing gate beside Wolborough churchyard

3 INDUSTRIAL NEWTON

Bank Street
From St. Leonard's Tower walk up Bank Street and turn right into Market Street.

Market Street
Here you can see the handsome tower of the Alexandra Theatre which you can see was 'Erected 1871' and the Market Hall behind. On the left hand side of the road, just before the entrance to the Cattle Market, you can see an inscribed tablet which commemorates this extension to the Newton Abbot markets opened in 1938. Turn left here by the sheep and pig pens under the multi-storey car park on your right hand into Halcyon Road.

Halcyon Road
Compare the houses on the west side of Halcyon Road with those on the east side. Turn right along Halcyon Road.

Knowles Hill Road
Turn left to ascend Knowles Hill Road. Here you can observe a variety of rock types used in the stone wall on the right hand side of the road. Turn right into Rundle Road, then left at Somerset Lodge and right into Seymour Road.

Seymour Road
At this junction you can see a Victorian post box set into a wall built of an unusual rock which is highly cleaved and of a battleship grey colour. The road curves leftwards by following the contour of Knowles Hill. At a left hand bend you will see a short cul-de-sac on your right marked 'Private Road'.

Footpath
Here you take a footpath to be found past the first house on the right. After a few yards you should pause to take in the splendid view over the Bovey Basin and beyond. The Bovey Basin itself is predominantly flat; its limits are indicated by the towns and villages on its margins: Bovey Tracey under Hennock, Chudleigh under Great Haldon and Kingsteignton under Little Haldon. You are standing on its south-western edge where Knowles Hill marks the limit of the Bovey Basin in this direction. Here too you have a good view of the Bovey Valley, a cleft between the granite masses of Dartmoor and Hennock which follows the line of the Sticklepath Fault and, in the opposite direction, of the Teign Estuary with Bishopsteignton and Teignmouth visible.

Immediately in front of you Jetty Marsh Lane runs along the foot of Knowles Hill, the Whitelake Channel leads up to the Stover Canal and, on an embankment above the marsh, a goods railway line runs to Heathfield (part of the former Moretonhampstead Branch Line). In an easterly direction you can see the Racecourse and beyond, farther to the east still, the edge of Milber Down.

Having pinpointed all there is to see here, continue along the footpath until you reach a long flight of steps leading down to Jetty Marsh Road.

Jetty Marsh Road
Bear right and cross the road at the busy junction, then cross again. On the far side look out for the signpost indicating a stretch of the Templer Way which follows a path beside Whitelake Channel. Follow the River Teign to twice pass beneath a railway line which carried the former Moretonhampstead line.

Follow the path to cross a footbridge over the River Lemon.

Now bear left beneath two railway bridges: first the old Moretonhampstead

A Book of Newton Abbot

line and secondly the main line, to reach Newton Quay, commemorated with a suitable plaque.

The granite plinth formerly supported a capstan (see illustration page 53) used to haul in clay barges which were loaded from carts of the Devon and Courtenay's Clay Company's workings at Decoy Pit. Sometimes you can see grey herons swaying with the reeds here at the water's edge. This point marks the confluence of the Rivers Lemon and Teign.

Teign Road

Now double back and bear left along Teign Road beside Tuckers Maltings on your left and Osborne Park on your right. Walk straight on to reach Queen Street and bear right. Alternatively, you can follow back streets by turning right into Osborne Street, past All Saints School, across the Avenue, along Albert Terrace, then follow Marsh Road beside the Lemon to reach Kingsteignton Road, Courtenay Street and St Leonard's Tower.

These then are three suggested town trails on which you can see much of interest around the older parts of Newton Abbot. There are of course many other walks in and around the town which include the footpath way. From Bradley Manor you can continue up-river through Bradley Woods towards Ogwell Mill Road and Chercombe Bridge. Ogwell Mill Road brings you back to Ashburton Road in the vicinity of Bradley Barton and Bradley Valley. Instead of taking Ogwell Mill Road you can cross the Lemon here and return on the south bank, perhaps taking a detour through the woods over Emblett Hill towards Ogwell Road. From here you can reach Ogwell Cross on the Totnes Road. From Coach Road you can take a footpath which leads across fields and through woods by the side of the flooded Decoy Pit to Decoy Road. From St. Marychurch Road you can ascend Milber Down by Milber Pine Walk and then follow Milber Lane across Aller Brake towards Coffinswell. Yet another interesting route can be pursued by exploring the Teign Marsh and Stover Canal area from the footpath which bears left from the Kingsteignton Road between the Canal and the Heathfield railway line.

Ordnance Survey Explorer Sheet 110 is all you need to explore these local footpaths as your fancy takes you.

A map of the town would be a useful companion on these walks. Indeed, Newton Abbot Town Council has been busy naming, recording and reinstating where necessary all public footpaths in and around the town. In 2005 a comprehensive footpath map was produced, copies of which are available, free of charge, from the Council Offices in Devon Square.

Bibliography

The two accounts of Newton Abbot to which I have referred throughout the text are as follows:
STIRLING, Rev D M.: *A History of Newton-Abbot and Newton-Bushel*, 1830
RHODES, A.J.: *Newton Abbot: its History and Development*, etc., c.1904

The Transactions of the Devonshire Association (**TDA**) are an invaluable source of information, although one must remain sceptical of the accuracy of some of the early papers. I have turned up every reference to Newton Abbot and Newton Bushel since the Transactions were first published in 1862. Some of the more substantial items are listed below under subject headings together with books, articles and unpublished papers which contain material relevant to the study of Newton Abbot. Further entries in **TDA** are referred to throughout the text and are quoted by their year of publication.

A series of articles on various aspects of Newton Abbot history written by the late Edith Wheeler and published in the *Mid-Devon Advertiser* during the late 1960s proved very useful.

Town guides, published by Newton Abbot Urban District Council and, since 1974, by Newton Abbot Town Council, as well as by commercial publishers such as Burrows, contain little information which is not already given in **Stirling** or **Rhodes**. Their chief interest lies in the advertisements they contain. Of particular use are the following:

CRESSWELL, Beatrix F: *Newton Abbot (Devon) and its neighbouring villages, including Chudleigh*; Warne and Co., 1908
WILLIS, C A: *Newton Abbot*, 1920

County Directories are also useful in tracing particular businesses and institutions. Stirling provides one of the earliest lists of persons engaged in trade and the professions. Various editions of *White's Devon Directory* and *Kelly's Directory of Devon and Cornwall* were among those referred to. In addition to the above, the main works consulted are listed below under broad subject headings:

History
CODY, Paul: *A History of Newton Abbot*, c. 1970 Paper deposited at Newton Abbot Library
DEVON NOTES AND QUERIES Vol 4, 1906-7, 'Forde House', by Roscoe Gibbs
FIRTH, Diana: *Bradley Manor*; National Trust, 1978
O'HAGAN, Mary: *A History of Forde House*. Teignbridge District Council, 1990
SEYMOUR, Deryck: *Torre Abbey*, 1977
TDA, Vol 12, 1880, pages 204-225, 'The Landing of the Prince of Orange at Brixham, 1688', by T W Windeatt
TDA, Vol 16, 1884, 'Notes on the History of Highweek', by Rev S G Harris
TDA, Vol 31, 1899, 'Notes on the History of Newton Abbot' by Rev S G Harris
TDA, Vol 68, 1936, 'Early Owners of Bradley Manor' by J J Alexander
TORQUAY NATURAL HISTORY SOCIETY TRANSACTIONS 1930-34, 'Teignbridge: a Chapter in the Early History of Newton Abbot' by Hugh R Watkin

Geology
PERKINS, John W: *Geology Explained in South and East Devon*; David and Charles, 1971
PROCEEDINGS OF THE GEOLOGISTS' ASSOCIATION: Vol XVI, Part 8, July 1900;
'Excursion to Newton Abbot, Chudleigh, Dartmoor and Torquay', Easter, 1900. Various authors.
QUARTERLY JOURNAL OF THE GEOLOGICAL SOCIETY: Vol 78, Part 3, 1922;

A Book of Newton Abbot

'Composite Sill at Newton Abbot', by W G Shannon

UNSWORTH, H: Notes on Wolborough Iron Mine, Newton Abbot, 1972; Paper deposited at Newton Abbot Library

USSHER, W E A, et al: *The Geology of the Country around Newton Abbot*; HMSO, Memoirs of the Geological Survey, 1913

Products

PARISH, C W: *The Creation of an Industry*, 1947

QUARRY MANAGERS' JOURNAL, August 1964; 'Ball Clay Production in South Devon'

ROLT, L T C: *The Potters' Field: a History of the South Devon Ball Clay Industry*; David and Charles, 1974

SHORTER, A H, RAVENHILL, W L D and GREGORY, K J: *Southwest England*; Nelson, 1969

ST. JOHN THOMAS, David: *Journey Through Britain: Landscape, People and Books*. Frances Lincoln, 2004

VARIOUS AUTHORS: *Good Books Come From Devon: The David & Charles Twenty-First Birthday Book*. David & Charles, 1981

THE VICARIAN, December 1928: 'A History of the Firm', by C L Vicary; Deposited at Newton Abbot Library

WEBBER, Jo: Tuckers Maltings, no date. Copies available at Tuckers Maltings shop

Trade and Communications

CLAYTON, Howard: *The Atmospheric Railways*, 1966

EWANS, M C: *The Haytor Granite Tramway and Stover Canal*; David and Charles, 1964

BEAVIS, Derek: *The Templer Way*; Obelisk Publications, rev. ed. 1996

HADFIELD, Charles: *Atmospheric Railways: a Victorian Venture in Silent Speed*; David and Charles, 1967

HADFIELD, Charles: *The Canals of South West England*; David and Charles, 1967

MACDERMOT, E T: *History of the Great Western Railway, Vol 2 1863-1921;* Ian Allan, 1973

MURRIN-PYNE, Naomi: *The History and Development of Newton Abbot Market*, 1972 Paper deposited at Newton Abbot Library

THOMAS, David St John: *A Regional History of the Railways of Great Britain, Vol 1, The West Country*; David and Charles, 1973

TRUMP, H J: *Westcountry Harbour*; Brunswick Press, 1976

River Lemon

CHANDLER, Chas H: *The Memorable Floods in and around Newton Abbot on November 14th, 1894*; Samuel Wotton, 22 Courtenay Street, Newton Abbot

John Lethbridge

HISTORY TODAY, December 1978, 'John Lethbridge, Diver', by Zélide Cowan

NATIONAL GEOGRAPHIC MAGAZINE, Aug. 1975, 'The Treasure of Porto Santo', by Robert Stenuit

TDA, Vol 12, 1880, 'John Lethbridge and his Diving Machine', by John S Amery

Church and Chapel

MARTIN, W: Keble Over the Hills...; Michael Joseph, 1968

TDA, Vol 16, 1884: 'Early Nonconformity in Newton and its Neighbourhood' by Edward Windeatt

Some of the Town's Institutions

DEACON, Lois: *An Angel from Your Door*, United Writers Pubns., 1973

LEY, J W: *Anecdotes of the West Country and other Reminiscences from a Devonshire Doctor's Diary*; Published c. 1890

Bibliography

Passmore Edwards and Newton Abbot Library

BAYNES, Peter: *John Passmore Edwards, 1823-1911: An Account of the Life and Works.* Self-published, 1994

BURRAGE, E Harcourt: *J. Passmore Edwards: Philanthropist*; S W Partridge and Co., 1902

EDDY, Karen: *The Beginnings of the Public Library Service in Newton Abbot*, 1970; Paper deposited at Newton Abbot Library

EDWARDS, J Passmore: *A Few Footprints*; Clement's House, 1905

Other items of interest, not necessarily cited in the text, are as follows:

BEAVIS, Derek: *Newton Abbot Past & Present.* Sutton Publishing, 2005

BERRY, Les and GOSLING, Gerald: *Around Newton Abbot.* Tempus, 1994

CARTER, Philip: *Newton Abbot.* The Mint Press, 2004

CHARD, Judy: Along the Lemon, Bossiney Books, 1978

DAVENPORT, Mary M: Newton Abbot in old Picture Postcards; Zaltbommel, 1984

JORDAN, Bill: *Paupers: the Making of the New Claimant Class*, Routledge and Kegan Paul, 1973. Account of the Newton Abbot Claimants' Union in the early 1970s

KINGDOM, A R: *The Bombing of Newton Abbot Railway Station*; Ark Publications, 1991

TOWNSEND, Elsie: Memories of Newton Abbot; Obelisk Publications, 1987

TOZER, Fred: Newton Abbot Album. Obelisk Publications, 1993

TOZER, Fred: Newton Abbot Album II. Obelisk Publications, No date

WATTS, Richard: *A History of Wolborough Hill School, 1877-1977*, 1977

INDEX
*References to illustrations are in **bold***

Abbey of Torre   118
Abbots of Torre   27, 64, 118
Abbotsbury   109
Abbotsbury House   105
Alexandra Hall (Alexandra Theatre)   37, 67, 68, 74, 108, 114, 142
Aller Brook   18
Aller Gravels   33, 38
Almshouses   127-129
  Mackrell's   26, 37, 129
  Gilbert's   127
  Lucy Reynell's Widows Houses   106, 128
Angel from Your Door (book)   130
Atmospheric railway   73-74, 77
Austin's   9

B & Q   9
Baker, Mr R H M   135
Baker, Sir Samuel   72
Baker's Park   135
Ball Clay   36, 50-58, **52**, **53**, **55**, **56**, 70, 71
Bark Mill   85
Beare, H. & Son   39, 107
Bearne, Maria Hannah   120, 125
Berry's Wood Hill Fort   13
Bibbings, Chemist   84
Bickford's Paper Mills   43
Blewitt, Octavian   33
Books   60-62
Bovey Basin   35, 36, 50, 57
'Bovey Coal' *see* Lignite
Bovey Formation   35, 36, 58
Bradley Barton   109
Bradley Manor   14, 16-17, **17**, 84
Bradley Mills   **41**, **42**, 43
Bradley Valley   109
Bradley Woods   32, 119
'Bradley Woods Bouquet'   84
Brandon, Lucy   18
Branscombe, Samuel   40, 41, 104
Branscombe family   40
Brewer, Charles   70
Brewer, John   70
Brewer, William   14, 118
British Ceramic Tiles   54
Broadlands Estate   109
Brooking, Richard   82
Brunel, Isambard Kingdom   73
Brunel House   61
Brunel Lodge   135
Buller, Rt. Hon Redvers   141

Bushel, Robert   15
Bushel, Theobald   15
Butter Market *see* Market Hall

Candy Tiles   54
Carnegie, Andrew   139
Carter, Philip, author   11
Castle Dyke   13, 16
Centrax   112
Chercombe Bridge   31, 32
Church Institute, St Mary's, Highweek   114
Churches and Chapels
  All Saints, Highweek   16, 113-114
  All Saints Mission Chapel (Railway Mission), Osborne Street   123
  Assemblies of God   123
  Baptist Church   106, 121
  Bible Christian Jubilee Chapel   **97**, 122, 124
  Christian Brethren   123
  Church of Jesus Christ and Latter Day Saints   124
  Congregational Church, Queen Street   **96**
  Gospel Hall   122
  Jehovah's Witnesses   124
  Kingdom Hall   124
  Methodist Chapel, Buckland   124
  Methodist Church   121, 124
  Mormons *see* Church of Jesus Christ and Latter Day Saints
  Pentecostal Church   123
  Philadelphia Hall   122
  Plymouth Brethren   122
  Pound Chapel   120
  Prospect Chapel   **98**, 123
  Salem Chapel   120, **120**
  Salvation Army   123
  Spiritualist   106
  St Joseph's R C Church   123
  St Leonard's Church   37, 118
  St Leonard's Tower (former St Leonard's Church also referred to as St Leonard's Chapel and Chapel-of-Ease)   **frontispiece**, 15, 22, 24, 64, 65, **117**
  St Luke's, Milber   124
  St Mary's, Abbotsbury   37, 114, 115, 123
  St Mary's, Wolborough   15, 16, 115-116, **116**, 128
  St Mary's Chapel-of-Ease, Highweek Street   **front cover**, 15, 16, 113-115
  St Michael and All Angels, Kingskerswell   123

156

Index

Churches and Chapels (continued)
  St Michael's, Kingsteignton 113
  St Paul's Church 123, 125
  Starkite Chapel 122
  Unitarian Chapel 122
  United Free Church, Courtenay Street 122
  United Reformed Church, Queen Street
    119, 120, 124
  Wesleyan Methodist Church, Courtenay
    Street **95**
Community Centre, Kingsteignton Road 115
Coombe Cellars 71
Coombe's Mill 85
Cornelius, Alfred 141
Courtenay family 24
Courtenay Park 106, 107
Courtenay, Sir William 21, 22, 118
Crawford, William 51
Cromwell, Oliver 21
Currying (leather) 44

Darracombe Beacon 34
David & Charles 60-62
Deacon, Lois (author) 130
Decoy 19, 57, **101**, 109, 112
Decoy Country Park 19, 58
de Englishville, Theobald 14
Defoe, Daniel 40
Devon Clay (book) 53
Devon County Council 28
Devon County Library Services 143
Devon Leathercrafts 46
Devonian Limestone 37
Doke, Gilbert 41, 43, 44
'Dream Church' *see* St Luke's, Milber 124,
  124
Drumclock Corner **91**
Dyrons 9, 115, 127, 134

Edwards, J Passmore 136-142
Emblett Hill 31
Encounters with the Past (book) 130
English China Clays 51

Fagan, Miss Eliza 125
Fairfax, Colonel 21
Farm Accounts Ltd. 50
Fellmongering 40
Few Footprints (book) 138
Firestone Hill 39
Firth, Cecil 16
Fisher, Mrs Emmeline 134
Flood Prevention Scheme 86
Floods 79-80, **81**, 86
Forches Cross 16, 63

Ford Grange 15
Forde House 18, **18**, 19, **20**, 22, 24
Forde Leat 19
Foss's Corner **93**
Foss's Island 108

Gaverock, John 17, 18
Gaze Hill 34
Geology 29-39
Gilbert, Sir Humphrey 68
Gilbert, John 127
Great Western Railway 77, 106
Green, James 71
Grout ale 49

Hackney 55
Hackney Canal 56
Hackney Goods Yard 77
Hadfield, Charles 60
Hangman's Hill 34, 84
Harris, Rev. 114
Hayman, Robert 128
Haytor 82
Haytor Granite 34, 38
Haytor Granite Tramway 58, 71
Haytor Hundred 14
Heathfield 35
Henley and Sons, cidermakers 44, 46, 47, 48,
  48
Hero Bridge 79, 85
Hexter, Humpherson and Co. 51
Highweek 34, 109
Highweek Castle 14
Highweek Local Board 26, 27
Holbeam Dam 86
Holbeam Farm 35
Holbeam Mill 69, 82
Holman Brothers 54
Hosking, William Henry 39
Hospital 133-135, **134**
Hospital Saturday 134

Imperial Electric Cinema **98**
Ingsdon Hill 34
Invertere Buildings 122

Jay, Kitty 129-130
Jay's Grave 129
Journey Through Britain (book) 61, 62

Keeton, Joe (author) 130
Keyberry Mill 15, 19
Knowles Hill 34, 38

Lane, Rev. Richard 16, 65, 67, 71, 104

157

Index

Lane, Thomas Veale 16, 65
Lane's Buildings 104
Leather 44-46, **42, 44**
Lemon Bridge 85
Lemon, River 33, 35, 79-86, **81**
Lethbridge, John 87-90, 115
Ley, Dr J W **132**, 133
Library *see* Passmore Edwards Public Library
Lignite 36, 58-59
Liming (leather) 44
Liverton 59
Local Government 25-27
Local Government Act, 1974 28
Loder family 82
Longford 63
Lyde's Meadow 65

Mackrell, Thomas 129, 135
Maddern, William 142, 143
Madge Mellor 9
Mapleton, Dr H B 135
Mapleton House 135
Market 64-68, **66**
Market Hall (Butter Market) 37, 65, 68
Market Walk 65, 67, 68
Martin, Rev. W Keble 123, 124
Masonic Hall 107
Mechanics Institute, GWR 140, 143
Methodists 121-122
Michel, William, Abbot of Torre 64
Milber 109, 123
Milber Down 24, 33, 38
Milber Down Camp 13
Milber Pine Woods 109
Mills Brothers Brewery 49
Minerva House 50, 67, 104
Monarchs
  King Charles I 19, 115
  Queen Elizabeth II 25
Morley Farm 35
Mortonhampstead branch railway line 57, 72, 74
Museum *see* Newton Abbot Town Museum

National Health Service 134
National Trust 17
Newfoundland Trade (Newfoundland Cod Fisheries) 44, 68-70
Newton Abbot Civic Society 10
Newton Abbot Race Course 80
Newton Abbot Railway Station 74, **76**, 77, 106
Newton Abbot Repertory Company 67, 114
Newton Abbot Rural District Council 28
Newton Abbot Society of the Arts 115

Newton Abbot Town Council 28
Newton Abbot Town Hall 28
Newton Abbot Town Museum 145
Newton Abbot Union 139
Newton Abbot Urban District Council 26, 27, 28, 123, 142, 143
Newton Bank 104, 108
Newton Bushel 15, 26, 27, 40, 44, 85, 130
Newton Quay 39, **53**, 68, 71

Odeon Cinema 117
Odicknoll Estate 90
Ogwell Edge-tool Mill *see* Holbeam Mill
Ogwell Mill 82, **83**
Old Priest's House 114
Osborne Park 107

Palk and Pinsent Brewery 49, 50, 105, 108, 122
Panorama Of Torquay 33
Parker, Mr 140
Passmore Edwards Public Library 27, 62, 136-146
Pearl Assurance Building 108
Pengelly, William 36
Pennin 9, 63
Pinsent, Mr John Balle 50
Polyblank's Iron and Brass Foundry 108
Powderham Park 33
Pubs and Hotels
  Bear Inn 103
  Cider Bar 9, 105
  Commercial Hotel **95,** 107
  Courtenay Arms 107
  Dartmouth Inn 69, 105
  Devon Arms 103, 129
  Globe Hotel 9, **95**, 103, 108
  Golden Lion Inn **93**, 104
  Greene Man 105
  Jolly Abbot 69
  Jolly Sailor 69, 105
  Market House Inn 108
  Newfoundland Hotel 69
  Passage House Inn 56
  Queen's Hotel 73, 107
  Railway Tavern 78, 107
  The Richard Hopkins, Wetherspoons 9, 10
  Seven Stars Inn, Highweek Street **front cover**, 105, 114
  Ship Inn 103
  Swan Inn 104, 108
  Union Inn 105, 117
  White Hart 105
Puritans' Pit 32, 119

158

Index

Quarries and pits
  Chipley 35, 38
  East Golds 54, 57
  Haytor 71, 72
  Royal Aller Vale 31
  Zig Zag 31

Radley, Mr W C 33
Railway 73-78, **75**, **76**
Railway Studies Library 145
Raj Belash Restaurant 103
Ransley Quarry 26
Reynell, Jane 21
Reynell, John 82
Reynell, Rev. John 22
Reynell, Lady Lucy 21, 115, 128
Reynell, Sir Richard 18, 21, 115
Reynell, Richard, of West Ogwell 19
Reynell, Thomas 21, 82
Ridgways (boot and shoemakers) 69
Ridler, Lilian 143-144
Roads (also Streets, Lanes)
  Abbotsbury Road 38
  Addison Road 109
  Aller Brake 24, 38, 109
  Ashburton Road 33
  The Avenue **96**
  Back Road 104
  Bank Street **93**, **94**, 104, 108
  Bradley Lane 41, 84, 104, 112
  Brunel Road 112, 122
  Buckland Brake 109
  Church Road 38
  Churchills 112
  Coach Road 31
  Coombeshead Road **100**
  Coronation Road 109
  Courtenay Street **95**, 103, 108, 122
  Cricket Field Road 38
  Decoy Road **102**
  Devon Square 107
  East Ogwell Road 31
  East Street 69, **99**, 105, 108
  Exeter Road 63, 64
  Fairfield Terrace 106
  Fisher Road 105
  Halcyon Road 10, **92**, 105
  Highweek Street 38, 63, **92**, 104, 108
  Hopkins Lane 69
  Jetty Marsh Lane 34
  Keyberry Road 122
  Kingskerswell Road 63
  Kingsteignton Road 34, 64
  Knowles Hill Road 34
  Limetree Walk 109

Roads (also Streets, Lanes) continued
  Market Street **94**
  Marsh Road 79, **81**
  Mill Lane 49, 122
  Newfoundland Way 69, 104
  Oakland Road 109
  Ogwell Lane **31**, 32
  Old Exeter Road 38
  Osborne Street 107, 123
  Pinewood Road 109
  Pitt Hill Road **101**
  Polyblank Road 108
  Pound Place 120
  Powderham Road 33, 74
  Queen Street 73, **95**, **96**, **98**, 103, 106, 107
  Queensway 109
  Rope Walk 69, 106
  Salem Place 120
  Shaldon Road **101**
  Shapley Court, Wolborough Street **99**
  St Marychurch Road **101**
  St John's Street 69
  St Leonard's Road 106
  St Paul's Road 107
  Teign Road 47, 106
  Torquay Road **98**
  Tudor Road 106
  Union Street 106
  Wain Lane 127-128
  Wolborough Street 64, 103, 104, **117**, 118

Sanderson, Murray and Elder Ltd. 43
Sandford Orleigh 72
Schireborne Newton 14
Schools 125-127
  All Saints Primary 123, 125
  Bearne's Primary 8, 125
  Bell's School 125
  Bradley Barton 125, 126
  Bradley High School 126
  Coombeshead School 127
  Decoy Primary 125
  Fordeleigh College for Girls 126
  Fortescue House Girls' School 126
  Highweek 125
  Hillside school 126
  Knowles Hill Comprehensive 127
  Marsh Primary 8
  Milber 125
  Newton Abbot High School 126
  Newton College 126
  Newton Grammar school 126, 127
  Science, Art and Technical School 126
  Seale Hayne Agricultural College 127

159

Index

Schools continued
    St Bernard's School for Girls 126
    St Joseph's R C Primary 125
    Wolborough 8, 125
    Wolborough Hill 126
Scratton Mr D R 133, 134
Seale Hayne, Rt Hon Charles 127, 140
Serge 40
Sherborne Mill 16, 85
Shute, Alison 62
Sibelco 51
Smith, Augustus Anthony 39
South Devon Railway 57, 73, 77, 106
South Devon Railway Trust 78
Starcross 74
Stenuit, Robert 88
Sticklepath Fault 35
Stirling, Rev. D M, author 12
Stockman's Mill 67, 85, 104, 105
Stoford Lodge 70
Stover Canal 55, 56, 57, 70, 72
Stover House 70

Tanning (leather) 44, **45**
Taylor, Miss Elizabeth 114
Teign Bridge 63, 64, 80
Teign Cider Company 46
Teign Marshes 80
Teign Valley Railway 77
Teignbridge District Council 24, 28
Teignbridge Hundred 14
Teignmouth 55, 57
Teignwick Manor 14, 15
Teignworthy Brewery 50
Telegraph Hill, Bickington 34
Templer family 70-72
Templer, George 57, 71, 72
Templer, James 70
Templer, James, junior 71
Templer Way 72
TESCO 9
Thomas, David St John 60-62
'Tiny' (broad gauge loco.) 78
Toleration Act, 1689 119
Tollhouses 63
Torre Abbey 14, 15, 17, 64
Totnes Turnpike Trust 26, 64
Treacle Hill 15, 64

Trevail, Sylvanus 141
Tuckers Maltings 50
Tudor, Rev. 106, 126, 135

Ugbrooke House 123
'Undercleave' (house) 31
Union Bridge 85, 104

Veale, Thomas 16, 65
Ventiford 56, 70, 71, 72
Vicary, Charles Lane 40, 43, 44
Vicary, Elizabeth 41
Vicary family 40, 41, 44, 134
Vicary, John 43
Vicary, Moses 41, 43
Vicary, Robert 41
Vicary, William 43, 141
Vicary's Mills *see* Bradley Mills

Wall, Rev. Frederick 16
Waller, Margaret 21, 118
Waller, Sir William 21, 65
Watcombe Clay 38
Watts, Blake and Bearne 51, 134
Watts, Mr J W
Watts, Nicholas 51
WBB Minerals Group 51
Wedgwood, Josiah 51
Whitelake Channel 56, 70
William, Prince 22-24
Wolborough Barton 15, 18, 31
Wolborough Fen Nature Reserve 58
Wolborough Hill 33
Wolborough Iron Mine 38-39
Wolborough Local Board 26, 28, 67, 106
Wolborough Manor 14, 15. 17-19
Wolborough Street 15
Wool & Cloth 40-44
Workhouse 37, 105, 106, 129-133, **131**

Yarde, Gilbert 16, 65
Yarde, Richard 16, 64, 113, 114
Yarde, Susanna 17
'Ye Olde Bunne Shoppe' **Frontispiece**, 105
Yeo Ephraim 69-70
Yeo, Samuel 69, 106
Yeo, Rev. William 32, 118, 119, 120